Club Drugs

Other books in the History of Drugs series:

Club Drugs

EDITED BY KATHERINE SWARTS

Bruce Glassman, *Vice President*

Bonnie Szumski, *Publisher*

Helen Cothran, *Managing Editor*

GREENHAVEN PRESS

An imprint of Thomson Gale, a part of The Thomson Corporation

THOMSON
™
GALE

Detroit • New York • San Francisco • San Diego • New Haven, Conn.
Waterville, Maine • London • Munich

LIBRARY OF CONGRESS CATALOGING-IN-PUBLICATION DATA

Club drugs / Katherine Swarts, book editor.
   p. cm. — (The history of drugs)
Includes bibliographical references and index.
ISBN 0-7377-1953-2 (lib. : alk. paper)
   1. Ecstasy (Drug). 2. Ecstasy (Drug)—United States. 3. Designer drugs.
4. Designer drugs—United States. 5. Designer drugs—Law and legislation—United States. I. Swarts, Katherine. II. Series.
HV5822.M38C585 2006
362.29'9—dc22   2005046160

Printed in the United States of America

CONTENTS

loss of consciousness and amnesia. Some rapists secretly slip these drugs into the drinks of their intended victims.

CHAPTER THREE: MEDICAL AND LEGAL ISSUES

FOREWORD

Drugs are chemical compounds that affect the functioning of the body and the mind. While the U.S. Food, Drug, and Cosmetic Act defines drugs as substances intended for use in the cure, mitigation, treatment, or prevention of disease, humans have long used drugs for recreational and religious purposes as well as for healing and medicinal purposes. Depending on context, then, the term *drug* provokes various reactions. In recent years, the widespread problem of substance abuse and addiction has often given the word *drug* a negative connotation. Nevertheless, drugs have made possible a revolution in the way modern doctors treat disease. The tension arising from the myriad ways drugs can be used is what makes their history so fascinating. Positioned at the intersection of science, anthropology, religion, therapy, sociology, and cultural studies, the history of drugs offers intriguing insights on medical discovery, cultural conflict, and the bright and dark sides of human innovation and experimentation.

Drugs are commonly grouped in three broad categories: over-the-counter drugs, prescription drugs, and illegal drugs. A historical examination of drugs, however, invites students and interested readers to observe the development of these categories and to see how arbitrary and changeable they can be. A particular drug's status is often the result of social and political forces that may not necessarily reflect its medicinal effects or its potential dangers. Marijuana, for example, is currently classified as an illegal Schedule I substance by the U.S. federal government, defining it as a drug with a high potential for abuse and no currently accepted medical use. Yet in 1850 it was included in the *U.S. Pharmacopoeia* as a medicine, and solutions and tinctures containing cannabis were frequently prescribed for relieving pain and inducing sleep. In the 1930s, after smokable marijuana had gained notoriety as a recreational intoxicant, the Federal Bureau of Narcotics launched a misinformation campaign against the drug, claiming that it commonly induced insanity and murderous violence. While today's medical experts no longer make such claims about marijuana, they continue to disagree about the drug's long-term effects and medicinal potential. Most interestingly, several states have passed medical marijuana initiatives, which allow seriously ill patients compassionate access to the drug under state law—although these patients can still be prosecuted for marijuana use under federal law. Marijuana's illegal status, then, is not as fixed or final as the federal government's current schedule might suggest. Examining marijuana from a historical perspective offers readers the chance to develop a more sophisticated and critically informed view of a controversial and politically charged subject. It also encourages students to learn about aspects of medicine, history, and culture that may receive scant attention in textbooks.

Each book in Greenhaven's The History of Drugs series chronicles a particular substance or group of related drugs—discussing the appearance and earliest use of the drug in initial chapters and more recent and contemporary controversies in later chapters. With the incorporation of both primary and secondary sources written by physicians, anthropologists, psychologists, historians, social analysts, and lawmakers, each anthology provides an engaging panoramic view of its subject. Selections include a variety of readings, including book excerpts, government documents, newspaper editorials, academic articles, and personal narratives. The editors of each volume aim to include accounts of notable incidents, ideas, subcultures, or individuals connected with the drug's history as well as perspectives on the effects, benefits, dangers, and legal status of the drug.

Every volume in the series includes an introductory essay that presents a broad overview of the drug in question. The annotated table of contents and comprehensive index help readers quickly locate material of interest. Each selection is prefaced by a summary of the article that also provides any necessary historical context and biographical information on the author. Several other research aids are also present, including excerpts of supplementary material, a time line of relevant historical events, the U.S. government's current drug schedule, a fact sheet detailing drug effects, and a bibliography of helpful sources.

Greenhaven Press's The History of Drugs series gives readers a unique and informative introduction to an often-ignored facet of scientific and cultural history. The contents of each anthology provide a valuable resource for general readers as well as for students interested in medicine, political science, philosophy, and social studies.

The drugs grouped under the umbrella term *club drugs* are not part of a single chemical family. Instead, the drugs are so named because of their frequent use at clublike dance parties, popularly called "raves." Most cultural historians agree that raves—events at which young people dance all night at a rented or makeshift dance hall—originated in Europe and only reached the United States around 1991. The Spanish island of Ibiza is generally credited with holding the first rave in 1983. Around 1987 British visitors to Ibiza—convicts on probation, some say—discovered rave culture and brought it home with them. "Acid house, a type of drug-fueled foreign dance . . . started to spread rapidly through [English] underground channels," reports historian Paivi Alasjarvi. "Small parties were held in mysterious places, and many people adopted the music as being 'their thing,' something new [and] exciting."[1] The summer of 1988, when raves seemed to be everywhere and were often held in the open air, would be remembered as the British "Summer of Love."

The idea of promoting raves for profit soon began to appeal to the entrepreneurially minded. By the beginning of the twenty-first century, raves were not just "small parties" anymore—they were big business. "Raves have evolved into a highly organized, commercialized, worldwide party culture," stated a U.S. government report in December 2001. "Rave parties and clubs are now found throughout the United States and in countries around the world."[2]

Rave Culture

Rave culture and club drugs are not inseparable. Concerns over the recreational use of MDMA, which most ravers call Ecstasy, preceded the development of rave culture by several years; sales of the drug were first outlawed in England in 1977 and in the United States in 1985. And drugs are not part of every rave experience: "You can achieve the same effects [a sense of pleasure and belonging] at raves without having to use drugs,"[3] notes one doctor. Even ravers who swallow nothing except water report feeling "high" on the atmosphere.

However, people who attend raves frequently do use club drugs. A 2002 East Coast study of nine raves—involving nearly two hundred ravers—estimated that one-fourth to one-third of interviewees had used club drugs recently, if not actually at the raves in question. "Twenty-four percent of the respondents . . . reported using Ecstasy within the two days preceding the interview, while thirty percent tested positive for MDMA,"[4] the report concluded. In fact, club drugs and rave music have similar physical effects, as the pulsating beat of techno music stimulates the same neurotransmitters (brain function controllers) stimulated by some club drugs. Hence, people who are attracted to one stimulant are frequently attracted to the other.

What Are These Drugs?

The drugs used at raves belong to more than one chemical family. Probably the oldest and best-known club drug is MDMA, which was first created in 1912. The drug is commonly known as Ecstasy because it induces "ecstatic" feelings that lower users' inhibitions. MDMA also stimulates empathy and warm feelings—hence its other nicknames, "love drug" and "hug drug." The physical effects of MDMA include accelerated heart rate, involuntary teeth clenching, and occasional muscle tremors. MDMA's closest chemical relatives are amphetamines (which are also used occasionally at raves).

Another popular club drug, GHB, is frequently called "liquid Ecstasy" but it is not chemically related to Ecstasy and does not produce the same physical reactions. While GHB does lower inhibitions, it is a relaxant rather than a stimulant like MDMA. Whereas MDMA accelerates the heartbeat, GHB slows it (though heavy GHB users may suffer scattered episodes of increased heart rate). Also, while MDMA users feel little need of sleep, GHB users may become comatose and, like heavy drinkers, wake up with little recollection of the previous evening's events. There are at least two other popular club drugs with effects similar to GHB's: ketamine, one of the few club drugs still legal for medical prescription, and flunitrazepam (Rohypnol). Ketamine is most commonly used—under strict regulation—as an anesthetic for animals and, occasionally, for humans. Rohypnol is widely known by the sinister nickname "date-rape drug" because sexual predators often slip it into their intended victims' drinks, knowing the drug will render victims incapable of resisting sexual assault or of remembering the crime sufficiently to report it to authorities. GHB and ketamine have also been used as date-rape drugs.

How Dangerous Are Club Drugs?

All club drugs have at least one thing in common besides being popular in clubs—they are widely feared as potential sources of addiction, crime, and antisocial behavior. The typical rave—seen by outsiders as a noisy, all-night party held for the purpose of losing control of oneself in a temporary and sometimes secret location with participants crowding in by the hundreds—is partly responsible for giving rave culture and the associated drugs a bad reputation. However, there is a widespread debate over whether club drugs are really "an enormous threat to America's teens and young adults . . . [which] cause significant health hazards, including long term neurological damage and addiction,"[5] as Drug Enforcement Administration (DEA) administrator Asa Hutchinson testified in 2002.

Some experts argue that an objective examination of the evidence indicates that club drugs are not as serious a threat as heroin, crack, or even alcohol. Most club drugs are physically nonaddictive, have few dangerous side effects, and stimulate friendliness and tolerance rather than violence, they note. Fatalities directly attributable to club drugs are rare.

Others point out that there *are* dangers associated with club drugs. First, as already mentioned, club drugs can be used to facilitate sexual assault or other crimes. Second, since most club drugs are illegal, there is no quality control of their sales, and alleged club drugs may be mixed with more dangerous substances. "Some abusers . . . are combining MDMA with heroin," reported the DEA in 1999. "If such trends continue, MDMA may become a 'gateway' drug . . . leading to the consumption of a variety of drugs."[6] Indeed, by the early 2000s club drugs—many of them laced with addictive drugs or other alien substances—were being sold outside the clubs and on the streets with increasing frequency.

Even pure club drugs have been implicated in tragedies. On January 27, 2001, Brittney Chambers of Superior, Colorado, was given an Ecstasy pill, in her own home, at her sixteenth birthday party—apparently the first time she had tried the drug. After swallowing the pill, she experienced a sensation of "freaking out" and drank some water, which seemed to help. As a result, she kept drinking more and more water—over a gallon in total, it was later found. Her brain tissue began to swell under the water buildup, and around 12:45 A.M. she fell into a coma from which she never awakened. The county coroner reported that Chambers had no other drugs—not even alcohol—in her system and that hyponatremia (water intoxication) was the immediate cause of death.

While extremely rare, several similar cases have been reported. Water can indeed help mitigate the dehydration commonly associated with Ecstasy use, but the drug also stimulates disproportionate thirst and compulsive behavior, increasing the danger of drinking too much water. While in such cases club drugs do not kill outright, it is almost certain the deaths would not have occurred without the drug use. Such incidents do argue against the frequent claims of proponents that club drug use is entirely harmless.

However, widely publicized reports of infrequent club drug–related fatalities, combined with a general public distrust

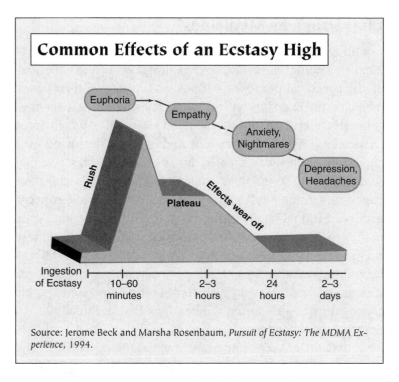

Common Effects of an Ecstasy High

Euphoria → Empathy → Anxiety, Nightmares → Depression, Headaches

Rush

Plateau

Effects wear off

Ingestion of Ecstasy | 10–60 minutes | 2–3 hours | 24 hours | 2–3 days

Source: Jerome Beck and Marsha Rosenbaum, *Pursuit of Ecstasy: The MDMA Experience*, 1994.

of recreational drugs, have contributed to the widespread perception that club drug use is riskier than it actually is. Even respected researchers have been known to exaggerate the dangers. In September 2002 *Science* published the results of a study, led by neuroscientist George Ricaurte of Johns Hopkins University, that indicated that recreational doses of MDMA could contribute to the development of Parkinson's disease. A year later, Ricaurte and *Science* admitted the researchers had mistakenly tested an amphetamine rather than Ecstasy. A mere confession of error did not satisfy critics, who claimed that Ricaurte had been prejudiced against MDMA from the outset. "In order to make his study reach the conclusions he wanted, [Ricaurte] had to ignore three previous published studies," wrote Rick Doblin, the founder and president of the Multidisciplinary Association for Psychedelic Studies. "He should never have made such bold claims."[7]

Club Drugs as Medicines?

Not all club drug research findings are as negative as those of Ricaurte's initial study. Most club drugs were originally created for medical purposes. MDMA was used as a therapeutic medicine for over fifty years; GHB was sold as an over-the-counter dietary aid until 1990; and even LSD—which foreshadowed the club drug culture and is sometimes used as a club drug itself—was created in 1943 by a Swiss scientist searching for a circulatory stimulant. These drugs still have supporters in the medical community. Even as public concern over recreational use led to most club drugs becoming illegal in the 1980s and early 1990s, many doctors still believed these drugs had medical value. "We do not believe that MDMA should be available for use except to physicians and to medical researchers," stated psychiatrist Lester Grinspoon and his colleagues in 1985 during the hearings that eventually led to Ecstasy's being outlawed for medical use. "But we strongly believe that MDMA has important therapeutic potential."[8] The drug's ability to relax inhibitions, they argued, could help patients recover from traumatic experiences by making it easier for them to open up to their doctors and therapists.

Proponents continued to fight to make MDMA legal for medical uses for nearly twenty years before scoring a victory. In late February 2004, South Carolina psychiatrist Michael Mithoefer received government approval to test MDMA's effects on post-traumatic stress disorder (PTSD) patients. Before the year was out, a similar approval was issued for a Harvard study on terminal cancer patients. It is possible that in the future, some club drugs may again become legal for medical use.

Whatever their future in medicine, however, MDMA, GHB, and other club drugs are likely to remain popular for recreational use. Consequently, the debate between those who claim that club drugs are deadly and those who insist that the drugs are harmless will continue to be contentious.

Notes

1. Quoted in University of Tampere, "British Club Culture," August 17, 1998. www.uta.fi/FAST/BIE/BI2/britclub.html.

2. National Drug Intelligence Center, "National Drug Threat Assessment 2002," December 2001. www.usdoj.gov/ndic/pubs07/716/mdma.htm.

3. Stephen Paolucci, quoted in "Ecstasy: The Facts," 2001, p. 9. www.ecb.org/pdf/SubAbuse04.pdf.

4. George S. Yacoubian Jr., Julia K. Deutsch, and Elizabeth J. Schumacher, "Estimating the Prevalence of Ecstasy Use Among Club Rave Attendees," *Contemporary Drug Problems*, Spring 2004, vol. 31, issue 1, p. 163.

5. Asa Hutchinson, Drug Enforcement Administration, congressional testimony given before the House Judiciary Subcommittee on Crime, Terrorism, and Homeland Security, October 10, 2002.

6. Drug Enforcement Administration, Intelligence Division, *Drug Intelligence Brief*, June 1999, p. 1.

7. Quoted in "Oops!—'Killer Ecstasy' Study Retracted, NIDA Credibility on the Line, RAVE Act Still Law," *DRC-NET*, September 12, 2003. www.maps.org/mdma/retraction/drcnet091203.html.

8. Lester Grinspoon, George Greer, James Bakalar, and Thomas Roberts, statement at Drug Enforcement Agency hearing on MDMA, June 10, 1985, p. 1. www.maps.org/dea-mdma/pdf/0103.PDF.

CHAPTER ONE

The Early History of Club Drugs

The Early Days of Ecstasy

Julie Holland

MDMA, commonly known as Ecstasy, was first synthesized in Germany shortly before 1912. For years the drug received almost no attention, but chemists finally began to study it in the 1970s. By the 1980s Ecstasy had become America's most popular club drug. Amid concerns over recreational use, the Drug Enforcement Administration (DEA) enacted an emergency ban on the drug in 1985. MDMA was classified as a Schedule 1 drug, illegal for any purpose, in 1988. (Since 2004 some medical researchers have received special permission from the DEA to study MDMA's possible benefits for the terminally ill and for psychotherapy patients.) In this selection Julie Holland traces MDMA's early history and the DEA's battle to make the drug illegal. She also describes the first debates over the dangers of Ecstasy and the growing popularity of the drug in Great Britain. Holland is an attending psychiatrist at New York's Bellevue Hospital and a recognized expert on MDMA. She has written articles about the drug for *Lancet*, *Harper's*, and the *Washington Post*.

Although MDMA (methylenedioxymethamphetamine) has been in the public spotlight only since the mid-1980s, its history extends back to the beginning of the twentieth century. MDMA was synthesized some time before 1912. The German pharmaceutical giant Merck was attempting to create a new medication to stop bleeding when it stumbled across MDMA as an intermediate step in the synthesis. On Christmas Eve in 1912, Merck filed the patent for this styptic [anti-bleeding] medication, called hydrastinin; MDMA was included in the patent application as an intermediate chemical only. The patent was received in 1914 and has long since expired. For this reason, MDMA no longer can be patented. Contrary to the stories of most reporters and even some scientists, there was no use mentioned for MDMA in Merck's patent application. MDMA was never marketed as an appetite suppressant, nor was it used in any way during World War I. Its chemical cousin, MDA (methylenedioxyamphetamine, an analog and metabolite of MDMA), however, was patented by Smith Kline French and tested as an appetite suppressant in humans in 1958. It was then abandoned because of its psychoactive properties; this is likely the cause of the confusion.

Between 1912 and 1953, MDMA appears twice in the scientific literature. Both times it is cited as a side product of chemical reactions, news that was published and received with very little fanfare. In 1953, the Army Chemical Center funded secret testing of various psychotropic chemicals, including MDMA, for their potential as espionage or "brainwashing" weapons. These toxicity and behavioral studies, which were declassified in 1969, were performed at the University of Michigan using animals; no human studies were conducted at that time. MDMA was given the code name EA 1475. Some people mistakenly believe that the EA stands for "experimental agent," but it really abbreviates Edgewood Arsenal, where the chemicals were synthesized. Eight psychotropic drugs were studied (mescaline, DMPEA, MDPEA, MDA, BDB, DMA, TMA, and MDMA) in rats, mice, guinea pigs, dogs, and monkeys. In late 1952, human studies using MDA were conducted at the New York State Psychiatric Institute, where a volunteer was inadvertently given an overdose of the drug by the researchers and died. MDA became popular before MDMA, in the mid-1960s in the hippie subculture of the Haight Ashbury area in San Francisco. Nicknamed the love drug and the mellow drug of America, MDA was reputed to impart a high that was described as a sensual euphoria that lasted for six to eight hours. Psychotherapeutic studies of MDA reported facilitation of insight and heightened empathy, but the drug was declared illegal in the United States by the Controlled Substances Act of 1970.

The First Studies of MDMA

Although MDMA did not become popular until the early 1980s, a sample was obtained in Chicago in 1970; it was finally analyzed, and the results published in 1972 verified it was indeed MDMA. Sasha Shulgin, the chemist who often is credited erroneously for creating MDMA, did not synthesize MDMA until September 8, 1976. The first published human study of MDMA appeared in 1978. In this article Dr. Shulgin and another chemist, Dave Nichols, described its subjective effects as "an easily controlled altered state of consciousness with emotional and sensual overtones." Shulgin, who lived in California and had many friends in the scientific community, some of whom were therapists, introduced MDMA to a few of his colleagues. He had had experiences with many psychedelics by that time and felt that this substance in particular could be useful to the psychotherapeutic process. One therapist, referred to as Jacob in [psychedelic researcher] Myron Stolaroff's book *The Secret Chief,* was so impressed with the effects of MDMA that he came out of retirement and began to introduce other therapists to the drug. This led to a slow spread of underground psychotherapeutic work in the late seventies and early eighties. Psychotherapist Ann Shulgin [Sasha Shulgin's wife] estimates that as many as four thousand therapists were introduced to MDMA during Jacob's tenure.

In March of 1985 Deborah Harlow, Rick Doblin, and Alise Agar, who referred to their group as Earth Metabolic Design Laboratories, sponsored a meeting on MDMA at the Esalen Institute in Big Sur, California. Several therapists who used

MDMA in their practices and other psychiatrists who used various other psychedelics were invited to attend. According to a [1985] article by George Greer, who attended the conference, "The combined clinical experience in using MDMA during the past several years totaled over a thousand sessions." Because of what had happened with LSD, which many researchers thought was a valuable tool but which was outlawed once too many people had gotten wind of it, most MDMA enthusiasts agreed to keep quiet. The media was discouraged from spreading the word, and very little was published about MDMA until a story broke in the *San Francisco Chronicle* in June 1984.

The name the therapists had given to MDMA was Adam, signifying "the condition of primal innocence and unity with all life" described in the Bible's account of the Garden of Eden. But MDMA acquired a new name among recreational users of the drug. It is widely accepted that the name Ecstasy was chosen simply for marketing reasons. It is a powerful, intriguing name to attach to a psychoactive substance. The person who named the drug, an alleged dealer who wishes to remain anonymous, had this to say: "Ecstasy was chosen for obvious reasons, because it would sell better than calling it Empathy. Empathy would be more appropriate, but how many people know what it means?"

MDMA Becomes a Recreational Drug

By the early 1980s, recreational use of MDMA had begun in earnest. A group of entrepreneurs in Texas, known to most as the "Texas group," started to produce and distribute MDMA in small brown bottles under the brand name Sassyfras, a nod to the naturally occurring essential oil of sassafras that is a chemical precursor to MDMA. Because MDMA was not yet a scheduled, or illegal, drug, people could order it by calling a toll-free number and paying for it with their credit cards. It also was available at certain nightclubs in Dallas and Fort Worth, Texas, where over-the-counter sales at the bars were subject to tax. All of this MDMA-fueled nightlife got the attention of Texas Democratic senator Lloyd Bentsen, who sat on the Senate Judiciary Committee and urged the Drug Enforcement Administration (DEA) to make the drug illegal. When the Texas group heard about impending legislation, they stepped up production, from estimates of thirty thousand tablets a month to as much as eight thousand tablets a day. In the few months before MDMA became illegal, it is possible that the Texas group made as many as two million tablets of Ecstasy.

The DEA published their intention to declare MDMA a Schedule I drug on July 27, 1984, in the Federal Register. A Schedule I drug is prohibited for every application, has no recognized medical use, and cannot be prescribed by a physician. In response to the DEA's proposal, a group of psychiatrists, psychotherapists, and researchers (Thomas Roberts, George Greer, Lester Grinspoon, and James Bakalar), together with their lawyer, Richard Cotton, filed a letter within the thirty-day period allotted by law to the DEA administrator, Francis Mullen, requesting a hearing. The request was granted, and the DEA scheduled hearings in Los Angeles, Kansas City, and Washington, D.C.

On May 31, 1985, the DEA announced that it would not wait for the hearings to be completed before acting, because their recent data indicated that the drug was being abused in twenty-eight states. On an emergency basis, the DEA "scheduled" MDMA, taking advantage of a law passed in October 1984 that allows drugs to be scheduled for one year, without hearings, if there is enough concern for public safety. MDMA is the only drug that has been scheduled in this manner. The ban took effect July 1, 1985. The emergency action was an interim measure to curb Ecstasy abuse until the longer administrative process could be completed. The DEA also initiated efforts to criminalize all aspects of MDMA internationally. An expert committee of the World Health Organization recommended that MDMA be placed in Schedule I but urged countries to "facilitate research in this interesting substance." The chairman of this group voted against scheduling MDMA and felt that the decision should be deferred while awaiting data on the substance's therapeutic usefulness. MDMA was placed in Schedule I internationally on February 11, 1986.

The First Government Hearings

The DEA hearings took place in February, June, and July of 1985. Many psychiatrists, research scientists, psychotherapists, and, of course, lawyers took part. People who had experience giving MDMA to patients testified as to the unique utility of MDMA to catalyze the therapeutic process, to enhance insight and communication between spouses, family members, and therapist and patient. Speaking on behalf of the DEA were those who felt that MDMA caused brain damage. Dr. Lewis Seiden of the University of Chicago presented data from animal studies of MDA, demonstrating changes in the axon terminals of rodents given injections of large amounts of that substance. Humans do not take MDMA by injection, but ingest it orally. Moreover, these two drugs are very different in terms of their effects and how long they last, and they have opposite active optical isomers. Nonetheless, the MDA neurotoxicity data seemed to make an impact for the prosecution's side.

To meet the criteria for Schedule I, the DEA had to prove that MDMA had no accepted medical use and a high potential for abuse. Unfortunately, the fact that no scientists had performed double-blind, placebo-controlled studies examining the clinical efficacy of MDMA hurt those challenging the DEA's move to schedule the drug. There simply was no proof, beyond the anecdotal, that MDMA did what the therapists said it did. Based on the weight of all of the evidence presented at the three hearings, thirty-four witnesses in all, Judge Francis Young handed down an opinion on May 22, 1986. Because he felt that there was an accepted medical use for MDMA, he recommended to the DEA that MDMA be placed in Schedule III. This would allow clinical work and research to proceed unhindered and would permit physicians to prescribe MDMA.

The DEA's administrator, John C. Lawn, was not convinced, and Judge Young's recommendation was ignored. During the course of an appeal by Dr. Lester Grinspoon (from December 22, 1987, to March 22, 1988, a period of time referred to affectionately as the "Grinspoon window"), MDMA was again unscheduled. Grinspoon won his case—the first circuit court of appeals in Boston ruled that the DEA could not use the fact that MDMA did not have Food and Drug Administration (FDA) approval as the basis for their argument that it had no medically accepted use. There were other points at issue. Congress gave the U.S. Attorney General, not the DEA, the power to schedule drugs on an emergency basis. The Attorney General was authorized to delegate that authority to the DEA, but the DEA acted against MDMA before the Attorney General had formally delegated that power. This intriguing loophole was used successfully by several attorneys to argue for overturning the convictions of their clients for MDMA possession and trafficking, convictions that took place before the permanent scheduling of the drug. At the end of all the trials and appeal, John Lawn and the DEA permanently placed MDMA in Schedule I on March 23, 1988.

Ecstasy in the Public Eye

As a result of the trials, the media got wind of the situation— "Miracle Medicine/Party Drug Goes on Trial" ran the headlines. Many questions began to be posed. Was MDMA an amazing therapeutic tool, as proposed by the West Coast shrinks? Was it a killer drug that causes brain damage, as promulgated by the DEA? Every magazine article and every television news story was free publicity for the drug Ecstasy. The so-called hug drug or love drug was a hot story in the summer of 1985. Indeed, that was when I first heard of MDMA. I remember feeling sorry for the psychiatrists who had based their practices on MDMA-assisted psychotherapy. How hard it must be for them when they had seen the benefits of its proper use. Many of these practitioners, not willing to risk their licenses and livelihoods to administer an illegal drug, ceased using it. But some continued, becoming "underground" therapists. As Ann Shulgin described it, "MDMA is penicillin for the soul; you don't give up penicillin when you see what it can do."

Some time in the early 1980s, a group of intravenous heroin users in northern California made national news when they inadvertently injected themselves with MPTP (1-methyl-4-phenyl-1,2,5,6-tetrahydropyridine), the unfortunate product of a botched attempt to concoct a synthetic opiate. In at least seven of these individuals, a severe form of parkinsonism [muscle rigidity] developed, with shaking tremors and impressive episodes of near paralysis. This made for amazing copy, and many television talk shows aired images of these patients on the same shows that were explaining the other popular drug of that time, MDMA. Because of this synchronicity many people became confused and assumed that MDMA caused Parkinson's disease. MPTP has been shown to be toxic to dopamine-producing neurons and is now used as a chemical model for mimicking Parkinson's disease. MDMA has never been shown to damage dopamine-producing neurons or cause parkinsonian symptoms.

With the increased media coverage of Ecstasy during the mid-1980s came growing recreational use of the drug. Several surveys of college campuses reflected this trend—anywhere from 8 percent to 39 percent of those surveyed admitted using the drug. In the early eighties, Ecstasy use in the gay club scene of New York, specifically at [clubs] Studio 54 and Paradise Garage, enhanced its cachet. British disc jockeys and such performers as Soft Cell and Boy George returned to England from trips to New York City extolling the virtues of the drug. Couriers began smuggling Ecstasy into England from America. There are rumors that the followers of Bhagwan Shree Rajneesh, an Indian guru based in the Pacific Northwest, were proponents of MDMA and may have helped lay the foundation for its international distribution, particularly into the Netherlands, where MDMA remained legal until 1988.

International Use of Ecstasy

Some researchers place the beginning of the rave movement on the Spanish island of Ibiza, where two tablets of Ecstasy were confiscated by police in 1986. Certain DJs from London started "spinning" at the nightclubs there in the summers of 1985 and 1986. The summer of 1987 was huge on Ibiza, with large gatherings at the *discotecas* fueled by Ecstasy and an eclectic mix of music. Paul Oakenfold, an English DJ, tried to import that sound and vibe back to London during the winter of 1987, at the Project Club [in Streatham]. Afterward, large all-night dance parties, called raves, began to be held in underground locations or in clubs, with a growing number of attendees taking Ecstasy. What followed thereafter, in 1988, was Britain's "Summer of Love," when the raves were held outdoors with thousands in attendance. Unfortunately, that summer also brought the United Kingdom's first Ecstasy-related death: twenty-one-year-old Ian Larcombe, who was alleged to have taken eighteen Ecstasy tablets at once.

The rave phenomenon sweeping the United Kingdom, which was considered the largest youth movement in Britain's history, was soon exported back to the United States. New York's Frankie Bones, a DJ and producer, brought the rave to the United States after visiting England in 1989. His "STORM-raves" began in warehouses in the outer boroughs of New York and eventually took place monthly throughout 1992, the so-called Second Summer of Love. NASA (Nocturnal Audio and Sound Awakening), a popular rave at the Manhattan club Shelter, kicked off in July 1992, and one of the first large U.S. raves in San Francisco, Toon Town, debuted in 1991. Raves are still going strong in the San Francisco Bay Area [as of 2001], and Oakland's version, called massives, bring anywhere from five thousand to thirty thousand attendees.

Alexander Shulgin: The Controversial Promoter of MDMA

Dennis Romero

Alexander T. "Sasha" Shulgin is known as the "stepfather of MDMA" and the "godfather of Ecstasy" for his part in bringing the drug to the public's attention. Shulgin's studies of MDMA began in the 1970s, and his work inspired much subsequent research—and recreational use. Shulgin is a former scientific consultant and expert witness for the Drug Enforcement Administration (DEA), but he lost his license to manufacture and analyze illegal drugs in 1996 after the DEA raided his California lab and found he was not in compliance with the stipulations of the license. The following profile of Shulgin was published in 1995, when the controversy surrounding his work was at its peak. The writer, journalist Dennis Romero, describes Shulgin's research on MDMA and the controversies it provoked. Romero, a senior writer for *LA CityBeat* and a former staff writer for the *Los Angeles Times*, has published numerous articles on nightlife and dance culture.

Perhaps it was a sign of things to come when a seven-story Monterrey pine came crashing down on the property of old Alexander T. Shulgin—Sasha, they call him—missing his musty cobweb-entangled drug lab by inches.

It could have been a good sign because the cantankerous

70-year-old wasn't around the back-yard workshop conducting one of his legendary experiments, which have been known to involve him downing any number of the new psychedelic drugs he invents in the name of science. Imagine losing your mind on some unknown compound with unknown powers (some of this stuff makes LSD look like Vitamin D)—and a tree the length of three buses rocks your world to Richter [major earthquake] proportions. The aliens have arrived!

Maybe, though, it was a sign of nefarious things to come. Like the DEA [Drug Enforcement Administration] guys who came knocking only days later, sniffing around the lab in search of improprieties. Or the U.S. Environmental Protection Agency people who checked out the lab that day last June [1995], taking notes while nosing around the beakers. (They found everything in order, says a representative.) The reds have arrived!

Thirty Years of Making Drugs

To tell the truth, Sasha Shulgin doesn't much care anymore what the government thinks.

He's tippy-toed around the law and the lawmen for long enough—30 years now. Since the mid-'60s, the tall, lanky, silver-haired chemistry professor has quietly invented drugs under the cover of a U.S. Drug Enforcement Administration license that allows him to analyze contraband so he can give expert testimony in drug trials. It doesn't exactly allow him to invent the stuff, though, and Uncle Sam appears to be getting cold feet about Shulgin's exploits.

But Shulgin's life's work is practically complete and he's ready to shout it out. "I feel the need of a public voice with some level of academic background. . . ." His message: "All drugs should be made legal."

With or without the DEA's approval, the public is now able to see pages and pages documenting all the world's known psychedelic drugs—many of them invented by The Man himself: the compound structures, the lab names, street names and, more importantly, what they do to people or, more precisely, what they've done to him and wife Ann, his 64-year-old partner-in-chem.

Part I, a book they call *Pihkal*, was self-published in 1991. Part II, to be called *Tihkal*, is due at the end of the year [1995]. The two books provide recipes for almost every mind-bending drug known to humankind. To Shulgin, the books provide scientific knowledge that proves drugs are a tool for the human mind. "The track record," he says, "is that there is great promise."

No one else on the planet has done more drugs, they say, than Sasha and Ann Shulgin. He is known for reviving the almost-century-old designer drug ecstasy, earning him the title "stepfather of MDMA."

"What he almost single-handedly attempted to do," says psychedelic supporter and Nobel Prize–winning chemist Kary Mullis, "was to chart out this whole area of compounds." Says psychedelic godfather Timothy Leary, "I consider Shulgin and his wife to be two of the most important scientists of the 20th Century."

Out of Obscurity

The Shulgins are legends among some academics—LSD inventor Albert Hofmann, now retired in Switzerland, is a friend. But they are little known to the outside world—they were never a part of the counterculture.

Shulgin's work has put him in the odd position of being a source of information for both the Establishment (during his decade working for Dow Chemical and his two decades testifying for both the prosecution and the defense in drug cases) and psychedelic drug advocates (his science has been used to bolster the cause for legal psychedelic drug research on humans, which is now taking place after a 20-year hiatus).

"There's nothing wrong with making information available," he says, legs crossed and drinking iced tea on his patio. The DEA, which repeatedly declined to comment on the Shulgin case, might disagree. The agency did confirm in a statement that it is attempting to strip Shulgin of his drug-handling license and that a hearing on the matter has been scheduled for Feb. 13 [1996].[1] And the U.S. attorney's office in San Francisco is keeping a file on Shulgin, although no charges have been brought. No one from that office would comment either.

Opposition to Drug Use

It's hard to find anyone with ill will toward Shulgin, although there are those opposed to the philosophy of his ilk. Psychedelic drugs are dangerous, opponents say—toxic to animals and dangerous to those who lose their minds and attempt crazy things like trying to fly. "One of the things psychedelic drug activists promote is that drugs are not a problem—that we haven't learned to use them properly," Wayne J. Roques, a retired Miami-based DEA agent and anti-drug activist, said in an interview last year [1994].

"That's one of the nonsensical things that they say," Roques said. "They seem to think it's a human condition to use psychoactive drugs and that's simply not so."

Shulgin's History

"I first explored [the hallucinogen] mescaline in the late '50s," Shulgin says. "Three-hundred-fifty to 400 micrograms. I learned there was a great deal inside me," he replies.

"That's a considerable experience," Ann says, puffing a cigarette and nodding.

Shulgin's romance with psychedelics started after [World War II]. He served his time in the Navy and finished school at UC Berkeley, earning a Ph.D. in biochemistry. "There was no mention

1. Shulgin was asked to give up his license and was fined $25,000.

of rebellion at that point," Shulgin says. "I was all smiles, open." In the '60s he did post-doctorate work in psychiatry and pharmacology at UC San Francisco and became a senior research chemist at Dow Chemical Co. He invented a profit-making insecticide, so Dow gave him a long leash. But while America's anti-drug fervor picked up, Dow found itself in the uncomfortable position of holding several patents on psychedelic drugs.

Shulgin left the company in 1965, built his lab and became, as he puts it, a "scientific consultant." That meant teaching public health at Berkeley and San Francisco General Hospital, among other jobs. It also eventually meant inventing more than 150 drugs in his lab. "To me," he says, "having your own lab is a very extreme pleasure."

Shulgin's Lab

Shulgin's spread sits atop a rolling, rural utopia east of Berkeley. The old brick lab lies down the path from his boxy white house, which sits on property that has been in the family for more than 50 years.

To this day his lab looks low-tech—lined with beakers, test-tubes, stills and pumps. It's funky but functional, like Shulgin. He wears handmade huaraches [sandals] with his tuxedo at special events and drives a '73 bug [Volkswagen].

Shulgin met Ann at Berkeley in 1979. Ann became Shulgin's soul mate, a fellow psychedelic explorer with a penchant for [hallucinogen] Peyote. ("I've read all of [peyote advocate and novelist Carlos] Castaneda," she says.) They were married in Shulgin's back yard in 1981. The man who married them, they say, was a DEA agent.

Shulgin and the DEA

As Ann put it, "Before *Pihkal*, we had a real good relationship with the DEA. They have few people they can talk to who are

on the other side of the fence who are honest." Says psychedelic drug activist Rick Doblin, "That was his Faustian bar-
gain—in order to do his work, he had to be useful to the DEA."
"It was not a quid pro quo," Shulgin says. "I make my research available to the government as much as anyone else."

Shulgin wrote the book on the law and drugs—"*Controlled
Substances: Chemical & Legal Guide to Federal Drug Laws*" (Ronin
Publishing, 1988), a book that sits on the desk of many law
enforcement officials to this day. "He's a reputable re-
searcher," says Geraline Lin, a drug researcher at the National
Institute on Drug Abuse.

Shulgin's First Research on MDMA

By the '80s, though, Shulgin wasn't famous for any books he
wrote or any drugs he invented, but rather for a drug he didn't
invent. In the '70s, a friend had suggested he check out a pill
that was going around called MDMA, or "empathy." He tested
it, tried it and wrote a lot about it in academic journals.

For better or for worse, Shulgin rescued the drug (known in
the lab as methylenedioxy-methamphetamine) from obscurity.
Invented around 1912, no one found much use for it until
Shulgin came along. He suggested time and again that the stuff
was good for therapy. The drug's effects are described as lying
somewhere between those of LSD and speed. "I still haven't
found anything like it to this day," Shulgin says.

But the drug found an empathetic audience in the nightclub crowd. Dealers renamed the drug "ecstasy" for better
marketability. And the U.S. government outlawed MDMA in
1985.

Controversies and Laws

A young group of scientists led by Doblin tried to preserve the
drug's legality, arguing that the stuff was valuable for un-
earthing repressed thoughts and memories. Shulgin assisted

the best he could, providing science from the shadows. But the government found that the drug caused brain damage in animals. "The one thing that is clear," says UCLA psychopharmacologist Ronald K. Siegel, "is that there is a lot of damage here with MDMA."

Shulgin says testing drugs on animals isn't worth dog doo. "There are real problems involved in testing a rat for empathy or changes in self-image," he told an English magazine last year [1994].

"In a lot of ways, Sasha was demoralized after MDMA became illegal," says Doblin, president of the Charlotte, N.C.-based Multidisciplinary Assn. for Psychedelic Studies. "It was the best candidate for legal therapy out of all the drugs he helped create."

 THE HISTORY OF DRUGS

Experimenting with MDMA

The following excerpt is from Alexander "Sasha" Shulgin's self-published book Pihkal: A Chemical Love Story, *in which Shulgin describes his experiments with different dosages of MDMA.*

Beforehand, I was aware of a dull, uncaring tiredness that might have reflected too little sleep, and I took a modest level [100 mg] of MDMA to see if it might serve me as a stimulant. I napped for a half hour or so, and woke up definitely not improved. The feeling of insufficient energy and lack of spark that I'd felt before had become something quite strong, and might be characterized as a firm feeling of negativity about everything that had to be done and everything I had been looking forward to. So I set about my several tasks with no pleasure or enjoyment and I hummed a little tune to myself during these activities which had words that went: "I shouldn't have done that, oh yes, I shouldn't have done that, oh no, I shouldn't have done that; it was a mistake." Then I would start over again from the beginning. I was

Shulgin's Work in the Late 1980s

But there was always Shulgin's trusty lab, which provided fodder for intimate trips with Ann and friends. Those times, up at his hilltop home, amid the rosemary bushes and live oak, surrounded by the smells of fennel, rue and bay, were magical, they say. "Inventing new psychoactive drugs," Ann says, "is like composing new music."

Sometimes, the music could be maddening. One time a friend, testing out a new Shulgin creation he called 5-TOM, became temporarily paralyzed and completely zombie-fied. It terrified the Shulgins. "There's no experience of this complexity without instances of difficulty," Shulgin says.

A few drugs Shulgin invented, substances with names such

stuck in a gray space for quite a while, and there was nothing to do but keep doing what I had to do. After about 6 hours, I could see the whole mental state disintegrating and my pleasant feelings were coming back. But so was my plain, ornery tiredness. MDMA does not work like Dexedrine [an amphetamine used to treat narcolepsy]. . . .

I feel absolutely clean inside, and there is nothing but pure euphoria. I have never felt so great, or believed this to be possible. The cleanliness, clarity, and marvelous feeling of solid inner strength continued throughout the rest of the day, and evening, and through the next day. I am overcome by the profundity of the experience, and how much more powerful it was than previous experiences, for no apparent reason, other than a continually improving state of being. All the next day I felt like "a citizen of the universe" rather than a citizen of the planet, completely disconnecting time and flowing easily from one activity to the next.

Alexander Shulgin, with Ann Shulgin, "#109 MDMA; MDM; Adam; Ecstasy; 3,4-Methylenedioxy-N-Methylamphetamine," *Pihkal: A Chemical Love Story.* Berkeley, CA: Transform, 1991.

as STP and 2CB, escaped to the streets of San Francisco. Amateur chemists read Shulgin's published research and made batches for sale. Like most of the drugs in his book, they were included on the federal government's outlaw list of drugs, called Schedule I.

"A lot of the materials in Schedule I are my invention," Shulgin says. "I'm not sure if it's a point of pride or a point of shame."

Shulgin's Rebound

Shulgin's rebound came in 1991 when *Pihkal: A Chemical Love Story* (Transform Press) was published. For fans of psychedelia, it was an instant collector's item. "I think *Pihkal*," Leary says, "is right up there with [Charles] Darwin's *Origins [of Species]*. . . ."

"The history of psychedelic drugs is still being written," says Siegel, who is respected both by the authorities and legalization activists. "Even though Shulgin's observations may not be entirely scientific, they are an important start since he's the only one who has made some of these observations and taken some of these drugs."

Pihkal, which has sold more than 15,000 copies, covers about half the psychedelic drugs known to humankind—the "phenethylamines I have known and loved," as the book's title suggests. The phenethylamine group of compounds includes such substances as MDMA and mescaline. The other half—a group that includes everything from toad venom to magic mushrooms—will be included in the forthcoming *Tihkal* [published in 1997]—for "tryptamines I have known and loved."

Shulgin's Philosophy

To understand the Shulgins is to understand their unwavering belief that these drugs have untold powers and that we, as a society, are ignorant of these powers—like early man who shied away from fire. Yet Shulgin's words are almost always sober: "I'm very confident that there will come a time when this work will be recognized for its medical value."

In 1992 he testified before NIDA [the National Institute on Drug Abuse] that psychedelic drug research using humans should once again be made fully legal (it was all but outlawed in 1970). Shulgin invoked his own legally questionable research on humans.

At the meeting, says Doblin, who was there, "he describes the work that he's doing with human beings, in a way that it's clear that it's illegal." Even so, Shulgin influenced NIDA's position that human studies should restart, which they did. "Shulgin put himself on the line," says Lin, who chaired the meeting.

"It was a scientific meeting, not a political one," says Shulgin, understated as usual. "I was explicit, but not provocative."

Later, Shulgin makes this much clear: "It's my stance that what I do is nothing illegal."

Laws on Drug Research

In 1986, the federal government outlawed research on humans using drugs that resemble banned drugs, called analogs. Before then, research using designer drugs that weren't expressly outlawed skirted the rules (using an MDEA compound [similar but not identical to MDMA] instead of MDMA, for example).

"Since '86, I've stopped all research in this direction," he says, i.e., he doesn't test drugs on humans. He adds that he still invents drugs and feels it's still legal as long as he has his drug-handling license. "I synthesize materials for publication," he says.

This balancing act is in response to the pressure he's been feeling from the DEA. It's ironic, say Shulgin's supporters: He has provided science to the government (most often in cases involving methamphetamine) and all takers only to be taken to task in the end for that very science. "Shulgin's not a criminal," says Mullis, "he's a chemist."

The Two Alternatives

So imagine Shulgin's consternation recently when he found himself playing a gig (he plays the viola with a local orchestra for kicks) at the nearby Bohemian Grove and club guest [former speaker of the House of Representatives] Newt Gingrich starts talking about . . . drugs.

Normally, this all-male club (the word exclusive is not exclusive enough to describe its clientele) is not so serious—the site of nude rampaging, mock-Druid fire rituals and all manner of back-to-roots male bonding. Snort-Snort. So when Gingrich started talking about a topic Shulgin has studied for 30 years, he kept his mouth shut and his ears open.

"He was very correct," Shulgin says.

"You have two alternatives: We either have to take Draconian means and break the back of the problem, or legalize drugs. I believe in the latter choice."

The Parallel Histories of Ecstasy and LSD

Tara McCall

In the following selection Tara McCall compares the history of Ecstasy with the history of LSD. She notes that both drugs were used in psychotherapy treatments before becoming popular recreational drugs. In addition, both drugs were banned when the public became increasingly concerned about their widespread use and abuse. McCall also examines how each drug reflects the era in which it was most popular. For example, she argues that LSD, which heightens sensory perceptions and interest in philosophical concerns, was the drug of choice for a hippie generation that valued self-discovery and peace-making. Ecstasy, on the other hand, is a drug that promotes feelings of empathy and connection with other people. The popularity of Ecstasy with Generation X, McCall asserts, symbolizes young people's interest in breaking down social and class barriers. McCall, herself a former raver, is the author of *This Is Not a Rave: In the Shadow of a Subculture*, from which this extract is taken.

Ecstasy and LSD have a similar history. Both had been synthesized well before the public or media became aware of widespread use. LSD was first utilized in the 1950s as a treatment for alcoholism and as a CIA interrogation tool. It is more familiarly known as the hippie drug, which helped bring upon its illegal classification. Similarly, ecstasy's first public use was in psychotherapy; once it became known as a yuppie and college drug it also became illegal. Today ecstasy is best known as the fuel for the rave generation, but LSD use at raves is also common.

In 1938 Dr. Albert Hofmann, a Swiss chemist in the Sandoz laboratories, first synthesized LSD 25 (lysergic acid diethylamide of the 25th compound), a compound he isolated from the fungus argot in an effort to cure headaches. Five years later he accidentally ingested a small dose of the compound and noted the experience as "an uninterrupted stream of fantastic images of extraordinary plasticity and vividness . . . accompanied by an intense kaleidoscopic play of colours." Hofmann had synthesized one of the most powerful hallucinogens, which came to be known as "acid" or "LSD."

LSD alters and expands human consciousness, increases bodily sensations, heightens awareness of color, distorts scenery and perception of space and time and initiates concern with philosophical, cosmological and religious questions which can lead, if the trip is positive, to an intensified interest in the self and the world. Psychedelics like LSD are sometimes disorienting by allowing one to access different thought processes. This disorientation is amplified by the complete sensory overload at raves. On acid everything seems a little more: lights are brighter, colors are more intense, sound has more depth. Although not for everyone, feeling slightly off-balance in an environment where there is no judgment can be liberating. It forces you to find structure and control in a beat and a rhythm. Many ravers combine ecstasy and LSD. This is known as candy-flipping. In this combination, LSD curbs some of the overly touchy-feely effects of ecstasy while the ecstasy maintains your ability to dance.

Hippies Reincarnated?

[Many have suggested] that the hippie was a precursor to the raver. Twenty-one years after the original Summer of Love[1] in 1967, English youth danced in remote fields and concealed

---

1. the summer hippies flocked to San Francisco to celebrate hippie culture

warehouses. It was coined by many as the reincarnated Summer of Love. Once again the media discovered white, middle class youth embracing new music, a new awareness and a new drug.

THE HISTORY OF DRUGS

Ecstasy-Enhanced Music

Ravers who take Ecstasy report that the drug promotes their enjoyment of techno and house music played at raves.

All music sounds better on E—crisper and more distinct, but also engulfing in its immediacy. House and techno sound especially fabulous. The music's emphasis on texture and timbre enhances the drug's mildly synesthetic effects so that sounds seem to caress the listener's skin. You feel like you're dancing inside the music; sound becomes a fluid medium in which you're immersed. Ecstasy has been celebrated as the *flow drug* for the way it melts bodily and psychological rigidities, enabling the dancer to move with greater fluency and "lock" into the groove. Rave music's hypnotic beats and sequenced loops also make it perfectly suited to interact with another attribute of Ecstasy: recent research suggests that the drug stimulates the brain's IB receptor, which encourages repetitive behavior. Organized around absence of crescendo or narrative progression, rave music instills a pleasurable tension, a rapt suspension that fits perfectly with the sustained preorgasmic plateau of the MDMA high.

These Ecstasy-enhancing aspects latent in house and techno were unintended by their original creators and were discovered accidentally by the first people who mixed the music and the drug. But over the years, rave music has gradually evolved into a self-conscious science of intensifying MDMA's sensations. House and techno producers have developed a drug-determined repertoire of effects, textures, and riffs that are expressly designed to trigger the tingly rushes that traverse the Ecstatic body.

Simon Reynolds, "Everything Starts with an E: Ecstasy and Rave Music," *Generation Ecstasy: Into the World of Techno and Rave Culture.* New York: Little, Brown, 1998.

Or were they new? Was the birth of rave a 1990s version of the 1960s hippie era, or was this something completely different?

LSD and MDMA were relatively new to the public sphere when introduced as the fuel for these two subcultures. LSD was banned in 1966 just prior to the height of public consumption, while MDMA was banned in the U.S. in 1985 after an American media frenzy over street use of the drug. In trying to decipher whether the drugs led to the scene or whether the scene led to the drugs, the inherent symbiosis becomes evident. As hippie culture became more accepted, so too did media and public discussion of LSD quietly subside. A similar development has occurred in Britain with rave. As rave proliferates globally and becomes more acceptably mainstream, public fears of MDMA slowly lessen.

Hippies and ravers alike claim that drugs offer the possibility of adding new dimensions and depth to their music. One commonality between the two cultures is the idea of "seeing" music. In hippie culture there was a hierarchy in the type of drugs used in music appreciation, with acid usually considered the most influential and mind-altering. The space held open by drug induction ("spaced-out") allowed for greater differentiation of sound reception and hearing manipulation. In particular, drug use allowed listeners to simultaneously follow the lines and sounds of different instruments, which was impossible for "straight" people to do. In some cases, acid helped listeners go inside the music: groups like Frank Zappa [and] Pink Floyd and guitarist Jimi Hendrix claimed that their music could only be understood through drug-induced listening.

Like the progressive rock of the 1960s, the aesthetics of techno are conducive to drug-induced listening and dancing. Because techno uses very repetitive drum and bass loops, some find it too grating or monotonous to tolerate while "straight." Specific genres such as trance use intensely high frequencies, layered sounds and intense climaxes to accentuate a psychedelic drug trip. Inversely, the drug trip accentuates the music. The use of samples sometimes alludes to drugs: The Shamen's

"Ebeneezer Goode" (translation: Es are good), Josh Wink's "Higher State of Consciousness" and Ashley's "Dope Makes You Feel All Right" are only a few examples.

Different Drugs for Different Times

Understanding the parallels between hippie culture and LSD and rave culture and MDMA, one begins to comprehend a key relationship between the hippie ideology of self-discovery, and the hedonistic rave ideology of collective empathy. Rave has given birth to what has come to be known as the E generation: a culture synonymous with drug consumption. Just as we can ask whether hippie culture was a reflection of middle America rediscovering itself, or discovering a new drug, a similar question surrounds rave. These sub-cultural evolutions were dependent on new drug experimentation and it is doubtful whether either scene would have developed in isolation from a surrounding drug culture.

Many would argue that ecstasy is the ultimate club and dance drug. Not only does it increase a taker's ability to feel music, it also makes those who wouldn't normally dance uninhibited enough to do so. MDMA emphasizes the physicality of music and mysteriously begs those on it to move. Initiating feelings of self-love, MDMA boosts confidence but not necessarily ego. It increases communication, collective awareness and empathy, making the dance floor a more electric, inviting environment. If the 1980s club environment with cocaine as the fuel was the "me" generation, the 1990s with MDMA as its fuel is the "we" generation. Generation X has been accused of being alienated and disenfranchised. Yet this generation didn't choose an ego-based, self-empowering drug such as coke; it chose a drug that would help people love one another, even if for only a few hours. . . .

Sexual, racial and class stereotypes and barriers are being challenged, while reservations and feelings of intimidation have been eased. Some have even argued that ecstasy was the catalyst in dissolving disputes between Protestant and Catholic ravers in Northern Ireland who united in the rave arena every weekend. Others have suggested that ecstasy has eased hostility between soccer hooligans. MDMA also seems to deplete sexual aggression, allowing dance to free itself of sexuality and participants to exhibit sexual indifference. The atmosphere initiated by E stands in contrast to the codified environment of most clubs. Ecstasy assists in the elimination of perceived social barriers and allows partakers to believe they can talk to anyone and love everyone. The drug helps to foster an environment that is open and non-discriminatory. Much like the disco scene a decade previous, gays are welcomed and are often prominent within the scene.

Acid house [synthesized, pulsating music] and ecstasy allow people to disappear from daily, mundane rituals. By inducing a more empathetic state, the drug permits participants to feel comfortable and free enough with their surroundings to express emotions to strangers. Straight males can feel uninhibited enough to hug and massage one another openly without fear of public scrutiny, while for females ecstasy creates an environment so unfettered by ritualized gender roles that they can hug males and even take off their shirts without worrying about being objectified and solicited for dates. The touching and feeling that MDMA initiates has given it the inaccurate reputation as an aphrodisiac. The drug actually increases the sensitivity of touch but decreases the libido and is therefore instrumental in re-introducing males and females as friends and not just possible sexual partners.

Ecstasy Becomes Illegal

Anastasia Toufexis

Ecstasy was prohibited by the Drug Enforcement Administration (DEA) in 1985, prompted by the public's concerns about the drug's growing recreational use and widespread abuse. The one-year emergency ban, intended to halt the drug's immediate threat to public health, was protested by a small group of doctors and therapists who felt the ban would keep a potentially therapeutic drug from being prescribed to patients. This selection was excerpted from a *Time* magazine article published the week after the DEA announced the ban on Ecstasy. Science writer Anastasia Toufexis reported on the facts and controversies surrounding the drug. She described the arguments of the psychiatrists and scientists who believed that MDMA could help patients suffering from emotional trauma. In some cases the drug had been used to help traumatized people discuss their fears and recover from painful experiences. However, Toufexis noted that other scientists argued that the drug caused unpredictable reactions, including involuntary teeth clenching and blurred vision. Toufexis is a former editor at *Time* magazine and has also written for *Psychology Today* and the *New York Times*.

Proponents claim that it delivers a gentle two-to-four-hour journey that dissolves anxieties and leaves you relaxed and emotionally open, without the bad trips or addictive problems of other psychoactive drugs. The Drug Enforcement Administration [DEA] says MDMA, or Ecstasy as it is known on the street, is an uncontrolled and rapidly spreading recreational drug that can cause psychosis and possibly brain damage. Last week [May 31, 1985] the DEA banned Ecstasy by labeling it with a one-year emergency Schedule I controlled-substance classification. That listing is reserved for drugs, like heroin and LSD, which have a high potential for abuse.

The DEA acted because tens of thousands of tablets and capsules of MDMA are being sold on the street each month, at $8 to $20 for a 100-mg dose. The drug, which seems particularly popular with college students and young professionals, has spread from California, Texas and Florida to about 20 other states, and its use has been accelerating in the past few months [of 1985]. Said John Lawn, acting DEA administrator: "All of the evidence DEA has received shows that MDMA abuse has become a nationwide problem and that it poses a serious health threat."

Ecstasy was prohibited under the Controlled Substances Act of 1984, which allows the DEA to ban a drug temporarily when faced with a threat to public health. In March [1985] the ban was used against the so-called synthetic-heroin drug 3-methylfentanyl. As a result of MDMA's classification, which takes effect July 1 [1985], both manufacturers and sellers of the drug would be subject to fines of $125,000 and 15-year prison sentences. Possession would be a misdemeanor.

A derivative of oil of sassafras or oil of nutmeg, MDMA is known chemically as 3,4-methylenedioxymethamphetamine and is not a new drug. It was synthesized [patented] in 1914 by chemists who thought mistakenly that as a relative of amphetamine it might be an appetite suppressant.

Today a small but vociferous group of psychiatrists, psychologists and scientists contend that MDMA has enormous therapeutic potential. Says James Bakalar of the Harvard Medical School: "I think the DEA's decision is precipitate. It's difficult to make a case that this is a serious threat to the nation's health or safety. They should wait until the research is in."

MDMA boosters cite case histories to argue that Ecstasy can act as a catalyst in therapy by neutralizing emotional defenses. MDMA has been used to treat patients ranging from a painter with "artist's block" to abused children. "In the proper treatment setting, it can lower a person's fear of emotional injury," declares Santa Fe psychiatrist George Greer, who has used MDMA with 75 patients. "A person can think about things, talk about things that normally would be too frightening to deal with."

In Massachusetts, Diane Watson, who was dying of cancer, took the drug under a doctor's supervision because she could not bring herself to discuss her illness with her family. Says she: "MDMA opened up a great emotional sharing." In another case, Kathy Tamm of San Francisco, who suffered from severe attacks of panic long after being raped, was able, while using Ecstasy, to confront her memories of the assault. As Tamm explained to her psychiatrist, "Not only did MDMA enable me to recover my sanity, it enabled me to recover my soul."

Therapists who endorse MDMA say that it does not produce the high of marijuana, the rush of cocaine or amphetamines (speed) or the hallucinations of LSD. Users, they say, develop a tolerance for the chemical and, according to some therapists, do not appear to become addicted.

Others are not so sure. Ronald K. Siegel, a psychopharmacologist at the UCLA Neuropsychiatric Institute, believes that reactions to MDMA are unpredictable and not nearly so glowing as some therapists make out. Involuntary teeth clenching, biting of the inside of the cheek, increased sweating, blurred vision and fluctuations in blood pressure have occurred during clinical sessions, he points out. Says Siegel: "People are trying too hard to make this drug into the one that LSD was not—a drug that is safe and effective and can be freely used and dispensed. MDMA is not it."

DEA Deputy Administrator Gene Haislip says that research at the University of Chicago has found brain damage resulting from a single dose of MDA, a hallucinogenic nutmeg derivative related to Ecstasy; the two drugs "are believed to affect the brain in a similar manner," Haislip said. Federal officials say that drug-treatment programs around the country have reported "psychotic episodes" among MDMA users. Even the drug's most avid supporters concede that there should be some limits on MDMA. They hope to persuade the Government to place Ecstasy in a Schedule III classification, joining restricted drugs like codeine [a narcotic used in cough medicines]. Says Harvard psychiatrist Lester Grinspoon: "The law would still have what it needs, but it wouldn't retard the kind of research we need."

The DEA has promised to expedite registration procedures so that legitimate research into the drug can continue, although therapists will no longer be allowed to give it to patients. Supporters of MDMA will be able to press their case at a series of hearings beginning next week [in June 1985] in Los Angeles.

Should they prevail, adherents would still have a problem. The formula for MDMA is available to anyone and cannot be repatented. Without the assurance of profits from exclusive production, no pharmaceutical company is likely to invest the millions of dollars it takes to test any drug for Government approval. Notes San Francisco psychiatrist Jack Downing: "MDMA is an orphan that has nobody bidding to be its parent."

Ecstasy Should Not Have Been Made Illegal

Ann Shulgin

Ann Shulgin is the wife and coauthor of controversial chemist Alexander Shulgin, who is known for studying and popularizing MDMA. She is also a former lay therapist who used MDMA as part of the psychotherapy she provided patients during the early 1980s. In this selection Shulgin reviews the history of MDMA use in therapy. She argues that the scientific community's failure to publish studies about MDMA and therapy was a mistake because such research might have prevented the drug from becoming a banned Schedule I drug, listed as having no known medical use. Shulgin also calls for people to have a more open-minded attitude toward the use of psychedelic drugs for therapy and personal enlightenment. Shulgin is coauthor of the drug reference books *Pihkal* and *Tihkal*.

When I first met and married [in 1981] Dr. Alexander Shulgin, known to everyone as "Sasha," he was still publishing his discoveries about psychedelics in the scientific journals. I had spent about three years working as a lay therapist, which means I had no proper credentials, no formal training and no reason to believe I wasn't nuts. I'd had no classic training in psychology, clinical or otherwise. During my first year of self-training, I sat with a few friends, a psychiatrist, a person who worked in state government, and then with a couple of patients

I inherited from the psychiatrist. We administered MDMA at the usual psychotherapeutic dose of 120 milligrams, often with a supplement of 40 or 50 milligrams at the one-and-a-half-hour point. (In a few special sessions, we used another drug Sasha invented, a psychedelic—which MDMA is not—called 2-CB, which has a clean, uncluttered effect on the emotions.)

I learned a lot. Every new person was a new universe, and I had to listen carefully with both mind and heart and be prepared to make mistakes. And I had to learn that, when I did make those mistakes, it was vital that I admit them to myself and to the patient as soon as I realized I'd been wrong. In other words, I learned a lot of humility.

All this time, of course, MDMA was legal. Or, to be exact, it was not yet illegal. It was being used by a great number of psychologists and psychiatrists, all across the country and in Europe. But since it was an experimental form of psychotherapy, completely unrecognized and certainly unapproved by the medical and psychological establishment, there were no papers published in peer-reviewed journals, and most of us didn't really know what other therapists, lay or professional, were doing. Gradually word was getting around, and at social events some of us were beginning to compare notes about the best ways of using this magical insight drug.

The second and third years of my work as a lay therapist were different. I met, worked with and then became co-therapist with an extraordinarily skillful hypnotherapist. It was the most exciting work I've ever done. It was also exhausting. Sessions would last a minimum of six hours, and if there was a need for extended work because something important was trying to break through, we would keep going until the breakthrough was accomplished. I learned to limit these sessions to twice weekly because of the amount of energy it took to concentrate on one person for six or more hours with no more than bathroom breaks and perhaps a quick bite to eat, remaining completely receptive and keeping one's intuition active and all one's antennae wiggling efficiently.

Educating the Scientific World About MDMA

In the 1980s, the legal departments of the scientific journals in which Sasha had been publishing his research got cold feet and his work with them came to an end. But we decided that this knowledge still had to be made available, especially to the scientific community. If we couldn't count on the cooperation of the journals while this new hysteria called the War on Drugs was obscuring common sense, we would have to get the information out in a book. We began working together on *PIKHAL (Phenethylamines I Have Known And Loved): A Chemical Love Story.*

There were no journal articles published on the use of MDMA in therapy. When the government decided to hold hearings on the possibility of scheduling [regulating] MDMA, all the therapists who had been using the drug had been postponing writing about it, waiting for the time when they thought there might be more receptivity in the professional societies. Of course, as we now know, this was a tragic mistake. If there had been just a few good papers submitted to the most respected journals, we would have been able to use those papers as proof that MDMA had "medical utility," which would have kept it from being slammed into Schedule I, where the DEA [Drug Enforcement Administration] categorizes drugs with "high abuse potential and no recognized medical use."

In 1985, MDMA was made illegal. I wasn't the only person who cried. This is a drug that for some clients could save months of time and expense in psychotherapy, a drug that allows insight into the parts of oneself that are unacceptable, unlovable and unbearable while at the same time in some way we still don't understand making it possible to see and acknowledge all these aspects of one's soul without self-rejection, self-hatred and self-loathing. This drug, I felt then and still feel now, could be the answer to Post-Traumatic Stress Disorder (PTSD), especially in the case of war veterans. Research on the use of MDMA in the treatment of PTSD is just now beginning in Israel and Spain. This is research that should have been conducted 20 years ago.

When Sasha and I began writing our books, I gave up doing the therapy sessions not just because MDMA had become illegal, but because I knew I wouldn't be able to give the best of myself to either work if I tried to do both. Now, having stopped doing this kind of therapy for well over 10 years, I can lecture in public and write openly about it, while fully trained and credentialed therapists who continued using MDMA underground can say nothing without risking a charge of committing a felony. A strange, new class of criminal: psychotherapists who refuse to give up using a compound that helps rescue strained marriages, traumatized victims of assault and rape, war veterans who cannot come to terms with the hellish memories that haunt [them] and people in search of expanding their spiritual world.

The Trouble with Calling It "Ecstasy"

I detest the use of the term Ecstasy for MDMA, as does Sasha. Not only has Ecstasy come to be associated with raves, street sales of questionable product and lurid disaster tales on television and in the press, but the stuff sold as Ecstasy is not always MDMA—there are, apparently, many people willing to risk the lives of eager young adults by selling them truly dangerous drugs under the name of Ecstasy. Also, the highest and best use of MDMA is in therapy and for personal insight, which is somewhat discouraged by noise and strenuous physical activity, like dancing. But considering that most large raves are held not far from big cities, and that the young people growing up in those cities learn very quickly to be suspicious of strangers, the use of MDMA at a rave is not entirely negative. Under those circumstances, sophisticated, street-wise young adults can let their guards down and for a few wonderful moments have a sense of euphoria and participation with people they've never met before. And euphoria is good for you.

Sasha is looking for tools with which to attempt an understanding of the human mind. (Not brain, but mind.) My search is a bit different. Psychedelics and visionary plants are, for me, tools for spiritual growth however you might understand that word, spiritual. My true aim in life is simple: I want to get as close as I can to understanding not just the human mind, but the mind of God, and I want to be able to live with what I find. I believe that every human being wants exactly the same thing, only most of us don't manage to articulate the wish to ourselves. We don't realize that that's what we're all trying to do. Psychedelics are my way, but they are certainly only one of a multitude of ways, all deserving of respect.

Early Medical Debates over Ecstasy

Marjory Roberts

On July 1, 1985, the Drug Enforcement Administration placed MDMA (Ecstasy) under a one-year Schedule I classification, making the drug illegal to possess or use without special permission from the government. As the date approached for the ban to expire or become permanent, the scientific and medical communities debated the dangers and benefits of the drug. Some researchers and therapists considered MDMA a potentially valuable psychiatric medicine; others pointed to research showing that MDMA causes long-term damage in the brains of animals. Due partly to legal battles spurred by the controversy, the final decision—to keep MDMA on the Schedule I list—was not made law until March 23, 1988. In this selection, first published in 1986, Marjory Roberts reports on the studies showing that Ecstasy can cause severe physical and psychological damage to the brain. She also describes research that suggests that Ecstasy is physically addictive. Roberts was a reporter for *Psychology Today.*

With a single twist on a chemical formula, "basement chemists" have sent legislators, researchers and psychiatrists into bitter battle. The latest round of controversy centers on MDMA (3,4-methylenedioxymethamphetamine), known as "ecstasy" to some and trouble to others.

A chemical relative of methamphetamine (speed), MDMA has been hailed by users since its street debut in the late 1970s

Marjory Roberts, "MDMA: 'Madness, Not Ecstasy,'" *Psychology Today*, vol. 20, June 1986. Copyright © 1986 by Sussex Publishers, Inc. Reproduced by permission.

as a "safer" psychedelic drug. Free for the most part of the hallucinations produced by other psychedelics, the distilled effects, users say, leave them feeling more empathetic, more insightful and aware. Some psychiatrists have spoken in favor of its limited use in therapy, claiming that it lowers patients' defenses, improving treatment progress. But there is evidence that even short-term use can cause long-term, irreversible effects on the brain, and other studies have shown MDMA's addictive potential.

Last year [1985] the federal Drug Enforcement Administration (DEA) took "emergency" action, temporarily placing MDMA on Schedule I of the federal Controlled Substances Act. Alongside heroin, LSD and marijuana, at this level of control, producers, distributors and possessors of a drug can incur penalties of up to 15 years in jail and/or $150,000 in fines [as of June 1986]. A final decision on MDMA's permanent scheduling is expected soon.

Concerns About Brain Damage

The DEA's decision came after consideration of a series of biochemical and behavioral studies conducted on rats and guinea pigs by psychopharmacologists Lewis Seiden and Charles Schuster. They found that MDMA causes long-term and perhaps irreversible effects on the brain. Serotonin (a neurotransmitter involved in the regulation of sleep, sex, aggression and mood), in particular, reached an alarmingly low level.

"We've looked at rats eight weeks after they've received MDMA," says Seiden. "Their brains are still depleted in serotonin, and there doesn't seem to be a hint that it's going to come back."

Without a government go-ahead, MDMA cannot be obtained for research or any other purpose. For therapists who had previously been using it in treatment, and for researchers wishing to study it, getting federal approval can involve a lot of paperwork and a measure of stigma, says Frank Sapienza, a chemist with the DEA. "Schedule I drugs are harder to get," he says. "And with this placement, MDMA would seem as bad as heroin or LSD."

Some Scientists Denounce MDMA

Seiden, Schuster and others, however, see these drugs as appropriate company for MDMA. "Its therapeutic use, to me, is completely unproven," says Sidney Cohen, a former LSD researcher at the University of California, Los Angeles. "There has never been a single article published on its therapeutic value. We have to ask why."

Psychopharmacologist Ronald K. Siegel agrees. "MDMA has been promoted as a cure for everything from personal depression to alienation to cocaine addiction," he says. "It's got a lot of notoriety, but the clinical claims made for its efficacy are totally unsupported at this time."

MDMA's acute physical and psychological effects resemble those produced by mescaline or MDA, another chemical relative, Siegel says. In addition to its "mind-expanding" properties, some users he has interviewed report side effects such as nausea and dizziness as wall as jaw pain lasting for weeks after taking MDMA. They also use terms such as "energy tremor" and "destressing" to describe their experiences, phrases Siegel says are euphemisms for muscle spasms and nausea and vomiting.

"I've seen people get ecstatic and I've seen people crawl into fetal positions for three days," he says. "When doses are pushed, we get madness, not ecstasy."

Based on their animal studies, Seiden and Schuster conclude that doses harmful to the brain are only about two to three times greater than the average street dose. This finding worried the DEA. "Seiden and Schuster identified a dose of MDMA close enough to street doses to concern us," Sapienza says.

The concern has spread to other researchers, who have been studying the substance for its abuse potential. Psychopharmacologist Roland Griffiths and colleagues studied baboons to see whether they would inject themselves with MDMA. When allowed to administer the drug intravenously at will, the animals did so at regular intervals. Since lab animals do not usually take to psychoactive drugs purely for their hallucinogenic effects, the baboons' behavior suggests that MDMA has some other naturally reinforcing properties, Griffiths says. Other researchers have found similar behavior in monkeys allowed access to the drug, findings they say should alert those who use MDMA recreationally or therapeutically to its abuse potential.

Although the DEA has until July 1 [1986] to decide on a permanent scheduling for MDMA, theoretically that decision has already been made. In February [1986], the United Nations Commission on Narcotic Drugs placed the drug on Schedule I of an international treaty that theoretically binds 78 nations, including the United States, to its regulations. This decision limits the use of MDMA in those nations to medical and scientific settings under government control.

Strict regulation of MDMA, however, will not prevent the creation and abuse of chemical successors. Researchers at the National Institute on Drug Abuse have already begun to study the effects of MDE ("Eve") [a chemical relative of MDMA that was legal at the time this article was published]. . . .

Without this sort of preventive approach, the MDMA story will be told and retold, with only a slight variation in format. "There's no end to the possibilities of drugs that can be engineered," Siegel says. "Designer drugs present a real law-enforcement nightmare."

The Ecstasy Controversy in Britain in the Early 1990s

Matthew Collin, with John Godfrey

Ecstasy use skyrocketed in Britain by the end of the 1980s as raves became popular with British young adults and teenagers. By 1991, however, both ravers and the general public were becoming aware of the potential dangers of the drug. The media began to publish accounts of people who had died or suffered from serious side effects after ingesting Ecstasy. The drug agency Lifeline published comics intended to inform Ecstasy users about how to minimize the risks of taking the drug. Controversy over the real and imagined dangers of Ecstasy grew. In this selection, Matthew Collin describes some of the controversies over Ecstasy in the early 1990s, including whether it could cause death or long-term physical damage to the body. Some people argued that heatstroke rather than Ecstasy itself was to blame for the death of clubbers, and that this danger could be avoided by avoiding excessive activity and drinking plenty of water. However, no one really understood the effects of Ecstasy on the body, Collin writes. He notes that during this time, it was difficult to find objective data about Ecstasy—a problem that was compounded by journalists who oversimplified information about the drug and reinforced fallacies in their reporting. Collin is a journalist with *BBC World Service* and has written extensively about pop culture and social justice.

Matthew Collin, with John Godfrey, *Altered State: The Story of Ecstasy Culture and Acid House*. London: Serpent's Tail, 1997. Copyright © 1997 by Matthew Collin and John Godfrey. Reproduced by permission.

It was . . . in 1991 that many [British ravers] began to realise that Ecstasy was not the miracle pill they had once believed it to be. People were ending up in hospital after long nights on the dancefloor. A few were dying, and dying horribly, with blood pouring from every hole in their body. The numbers were minuscule, but the perception of Ecstasy as a safe recreational drug was being seriously questioned for the first time.

The sporadic fatalities that had occurred in 1988 and 1989, which had been viewed as freak accidents and largely dismissed by clubbers who wanted to believe that "their" drug was innocent, now seemed to form some kind of emerging pattern. Talk in clubs was about mouth ulcers, blackouts, confusion and depression, projectile vomit, creaking joints, aching guts and unusual bowel movements. The finger was pointed at dealers and manufacturers, who were accused of cutting pills with everything from heroin to rat poison. While it was undoubtedly true that Ecstasy was being adulterated with what later transpired were harmless substances, it was also in 1991 that MDA began to reappear on the nocturnal marketplace. Compared to its chemical cousin MDMA, it was a heavy-duty experience—clubbers called it "smacky," erroneously believing that its exaggerated impact derived from some kind of heroin concoction—and could sometimes incapacitate the body. The influx of MDA "Snowballs" resulted in squatting rows of cabbaged clubbers clinging desperately onto walls: *monged out.* "Es are not as good as they used to be," was the collective moan that echoed around the dancehalls.

The first journalist to take stock of the changing mood was Mandi James, who had witnessed Ecstasy turning to excess, nights out evolving into sleepless, psychotropic weekends of what could only be called abuse, in her hometown of Manchester. In *The Face* in November 1991, she attempted to gather the sum knowledge on the health risks of Ecstasy use in Britain at the time. It didn't amount to much. "Never before have there been so many people going to clubs, so many people consuming drugs about which we really know very little," she wrote. It was the first time that any youth magazine had uttered what had previously been considered a heresy in club circles—that Ecstasy could be detrimental to health—but apart from common-sense information about scoring from reliable sources and replacing body fluids that had been sweated out in hot club environments, all James was able to conclude was: *slow down*.

The year before, Manchester drug agency Lifeline had issued the first edition of its drug-awareness comic *E by Gum!*, featuring cartoon hero Peanut Pete, a pop-eyed scally perennially buzzing off his nut, pulling on a spliff [a joint] and simultaneously dispensing no-nonsense advice. Lifeline coupled cutting-edge drug knowledge with a harsh realist outlook untainted by romanticism about "counterculture" or "consciousness expansion." Within a few years, it would become as much a part of the fabric of club culture as DJs, and its propagation of self-preservation rituals through the dance media would undoubtedly save lives.

The idea for *E by Gum!* had come out of *Smack in the Eye*, a comic for heroin users that Lifeline had produced in 1987. The strip was designed as a *Furry Freak Brothers*–style underground comic and employed the black humour and street vernacular of the user to get information across without sermonising. At the time, its explicitness was a radical departure. "We were interviewed by the Director of Public Prosecutions twice and several other drugs agencies wrote to the Department of Health trying to get our funding stopped," recalls its designer Mike Linnell. "We expected the flak to come from the media, but all the criticism came from the professionals." Lifeline's philosophy was "harm reduction": accepting that people were going to take drugs whatever they were told, and that the only reasonable response was to minimise the risks. Initially this meant needle exchange schemes and methadone maintenance prescriptions to minimise the spread of AIDS among heroin injectors.

When the first reports about acid house began to filter through to the drug agencies, they hadn't known how to respond. In the eighties, the key issue was heroin addiction and

HIV, and Ecstasy was a qualitatively different drug than they had experienced, used by a group of people they had never come into contact with. Their initial response, if any, was to view it in terms of HIV risk, to hand out condoms and advise people to practise safe sex. Ecstasy, they had heard, was a love drug. Still focused on opiate dependency, the only additional information they could offer was legal—the reminder that this was a Class A substance [that requires the strongest legal penalties], and possession could mean prison. Now Lifeline and others had begun to apply harm-reduction thinking to Ecstasy users, yet, for all its success, *E by Gum!* had next to nothing to say about the drug itself. "One of the most interesting things about Ecstasy," the text shrugged, "is how little we know about it."

There had been moral panics over MDMA when the scene first took hold in 1988 and 1989, but since then, the newspapers seemed to have forgotten about Ecstasy and its culture altogether, or perhaps believed that it had been neutered when the illegal raves were contained in legitimate venues after the Entertainments (Increased Penalties) Act [which governs offenses related to dance-hall licensing]. In June 1991, the multi-million-selling right-wing tabloid, *The Sun*, had even declared that "rave is all the fave," publishing a four-page pull-out guide to the "hot dance craze," which instructed, at the height of hardcore mania: "Forget the shock and horror of acid house. Raving is about good, clean fun. . . . Drugs of any kind are considered to be very uncool."

The first wave of harm-reduction leaflets, compounded by Mandi James's article, reactivated the panic, throwing the tabloids into a frenzy of scare stories, vilification and abuse directed at Ecstasy users and harm-reduction advocates alike, ranting and screaming about a nation's youth, as one headline put it, "In the Grip of E." Coroners' reports were unearthed and galleries of dead Ecstasy users' portraits paraded, the drug agencies excoriated for "telling kids it's OK to use the killer drug." Ultimately questions were tabled in Parliament. Conservative MP [member of Parliament] Gerald Howarth demanded that the Home Secretary withdraw funding from Release, which had published a leaflet on harm reduction, "until such time as it sends a clear message to young people about drugs—namely 'no, no, no.'"

The alarm was redoubled in the summer of 1992, when a doctor at the National Poisons Unit, John Henry, published two papers in medical journals, one of which was sensationally titled *Ecstasy and the Dance of Death*. Henry and his colleagues had been inspired to investigate after a "striking increase" in inquiries about the drug to the Poisons Unit during 1991. His analysis of seven MDMA fatalities armed the tabloids with a cornucopia of toxic reactions to the drug: extreme temperatures, convulsions, blood clotting disorders, muscle breakdown, kidney failure, liver problems, jaundice. "Ecstasy is widely misrepresented as being safe," he noted, going on to warn that the deaths, however small in number, might be an indication of a far worse catastrophe in the future. "These few people who have died are tragic, but the critical factor is the possibility of long-term damage. What we have going on at the moment is a massive experiment, and we will only know the full answer in years to come."

Ecstasy and Heatstroke

Henry's theory, which was immediately accepted by all but a minority, was that people dancing all night in hot, crowded environments, sweating out body fluids and not replenishing them, were in danger of overheating and death: the symptoms of heatstroke. The picture of a grey-suited, stern uncle, Henry delivered the catchphrase that he would repeat again and again over the coming years: "Taking Ecstasy is like playing Russian roulette." However, even though dance magazine *Mixmag* felt concerned enough to question, "Has the nightmare finally begun?" Ecstasy-equals-death was not a message that clubbers wanted to hear. It was generally rejected as anti-drug propaganda: unthinkable, impossible, another con trick from an establishment whose drug policy made no distinction between heroin and MDMA (while embracing alcohol and nicotine) and the summit of whose reasoning was "just say no"—not to mention a tabloid press whose currency was misinformation and lies. Ecstasy would breed a generation of cabbages—wasn't that what they had said about LSD in the sixties? They should try some themselves, that would chill them out a bit, it was often said. Then they'd know the score.

Whatever his agenda, John Henry had offered the first coherent explanation for Ecstasy deaths. At last there was a proper medical syndrome—heatstroke—and clubbers could ease their fears with the reassurance that the dangers of overdoing it could be avoided. Liaising with the Poisons Unit, the drug agencies had already started to offer guidelines for minimising the risk of dehydration, including the advice to drink "about a pint of water every hour." Keep cool, don't overexert yourself and you'll be OK, was the message.

Armed with the first hard medical information about Ecstasy use in the UK, the agencies began to target the clubs themselves. Leeds City Council had already introduced special conditions for clubs that included a supply of free tap water, and in January 1993, with the backing of Manchester City Council, Lifeline launched its Safer Dancing Campaign. The Campaign's code of conduct included the monitoring of temperature and air quality, chill-out areas, cold water taps and the provision of drug risk information. For clubbers long used to venues that resembled overpopulated greenhouses with only expensive bottled water for relief, such guidelines were a long overdue triumph for common sense. Finally, chorused agencies and clubbers in unison, something was being achieved: safer environments for Ecstasy use. And with the message hitting home, concern shifted to the drug itself.

In October 1993, *Time Out* ran a feature that articulated the predominant preoccupation of that year—the fact that what was being sold as Ecstasy was rarely MDMA. "Thousands of lives are at risk as spiked Ecstasy tablets flood the capital," warned the magazine. By this time there was as much MDA and MDEA on the market as MDMA. Concern was raised about whether either drug might be more dangerous, but the central anxiety surrounded the issue of "dodgy gear." "Drug agency workers believe that adulteration with heroin, LSD and even crushed glass and rat poison will eventually force casual users to shun the drug because of horrific side-effects," suggested *Time Out*. The crushed glass scare story proved to be based on an unreliable anecdote, and the heroin information was only half right: heroin had never been found in tablets that contained MDMA; it had, however, been found in a handful of pills designed to simulate Ecstasy that included other substances such as ephedrine. The article touched on the clubland paranoia of the time, reinforcing the commonly held beliefs of Ecstasy users themselves—that contaminated pills, not MDMA itself, were dangerous.

It took three deaths at the Ayr [a town in Scotland] club Hangar 13 the following year for this belief to be brought into doubt. These were the first Ecstasy-related fatalities in Scotland, and they shocked clubbers and drug agencies into a panic of speculation. Rogue batches of Ecstasy cut with ketamine and other impurities, the ingestion of GHB, the suggestion that MDA was some kind of "killer Ecstasy"; all were cited as possible causes. Some sensationalist reports blamed it on the "macho" Scottish rave scene, painting the club as a kind of disco death camp where bare-chested teenage schemies necked handfuls of Es on top of wraps of speed, Temazepam "jellies" and bottles of cheap, strong Buckfast tonic wine, inflaming themselves to the borders of oblivion with a brutal techno din. There was a collective refusal to believe that Ecstasy, the miracle drug, the innocent empathogen of Californian dream and acid house Summers of Love, could have been the cause of death. And yet at the subsequent inquiry into the deaths, it was revealed that all three dead youths had taken MDMA.

The truth was that received wisdom about Ecstasy was little more than a collage of unproven suppositions, prejudices, vested interests and misinformation, often amplified by journalists who recycled fallacies and oversimplifications from each other's articles as if they were gospel. The intricate nuances and grey areas of scientific debate hardly made for definitive and thrilling news copy, as one British doctor noted: "Most people want an answer. I've talked to a lot of people in the media, and they want to know, is it safe or is it not safe? Is it safer than alcohol, or is alcohol more dangerous? Is it safer than tobacco? And these are questions which we simply can't answer. Science isn't black and white."

Questions and Uncertainties

Could Ecstasy really kill, or was heatstroke to blame? Did it cause some kind of irrevocable brain damage? No one could even agree on how many people had died through Ecstasy use. Some, gleaning their information from press cuttings and coroners' reports, suggested it was around sixty in ten years, and that the chance of death, if it was assumed that half a million pills were consumed per week, was one in millions. Others, like John Henry, insisted the fatalities ran at nearly fifty *per year*; it was just that many were not reported. Others disputed the amount of Es consumed; the figure was less, they insisted, or more. And what about the people who were physically damaged but didn't die? How did they figure in the calculations? Nobody really had a clue.

There was more consensus on the question of why exactly people died after taking MDMA. Of the Ecstasy-related deaths in Britain, most had displayed the same heatstroke-like symptoms: fits, loss of consciousness, unusually high body temperatures, muscle disintegration, sometimes liver damage and kidney failure, and what is known as "disseminated introvascular coagulation," when the blood loses its ability to clot and the victim suffers uncontrollable internal bleeding, blood filling the body and pouring out of every orifice, including the eyes:

a complete system breakdown. The second explanation was an idiosyncratic reaction—that some people might have a susceptibility to the drug, and that one person's normal dose was their overdose. Water intoxication, or "dilutional hyponatremia," was a third, additional explanation, advanced after three Ecstasy casualties were found to have drunk large amounts of fluid, diluting the blood, swelling the brain and thus causing death. This hypothesis caused drug agencies to swiftly rethink their advice about drinking a pint of water per hour; it appeared that some clubbers, like twenty-year-old Andrew Naylor from Derby, who drank twenty-six pints of water before expiring, were taking their advice a little too seriously. "Water is an antidote to heatstroke, not Ecstasy," became Lifeline's new slogan.

Despite the folk myths that resounded through clubland, there was, however, no evidence that anyone had died as a result of taking contaminated Ecstasy. Although, by the mid-nineties, only about 40 per cent of the pills in circulation were actually MDMA (the rest were mainly MDA or MDEA, plus a few ketamine/ephedrine/amphetamine fakes), no toxic disasters had been unearthed, confirmed the police forensic laboratory at Aldermaston. Nevertheless, words like "contamination" and "adulteration" were still bandied about, both by clubbers who felt that "real E" couldn't kill and by anti-drugs propagandists who believed the scare would put people off taking Ecstasy.

Questioning the Mental Effects

But if no one really knew what Ecstasy did to the body, how could they quantify its effects on the mind? This was, after all, a chemical that had been popular among therapists for its ability to break down psychological barriers. What would happen when huge numbers of people took huge amounts of it for years on end—would those defences crumble forever? Each successive generation of initiates developed its own oral history of mental deterioration, of Ecstasy casualties "losing it," having nervous breakdowns, being institutionalised, even committing suicide. Were these just people who were halfway to insanity already, and the long sleepless weekends had simply pushed them over the line? Was the drug itself to blame? Or was it just a way to explain away the inexplicable?

In 1991, the first reports of paranoid psychosis and depression began to appear in British medical journals. While these featured a handful of individual cases, mainly people who were already psychotic and bingeing to excess, drug agencies also began to take calls from clubbers reporting moodiness and weird psychological states. Dr Karl Jansen of London's Maudsley Hospital, a specialist in drug-related psychiatric problems, suggested that "everybody who takes a lot of E is going to punch holes in the wall between consciousness and unconsciousness because of the nature of the drug. If you take a drug that is an emotional releaser, and do that repeatedly, then you are going to bring about some psychological changes." And yet, he qualified, mental hospitals were not full of Ecstasy casualties. Check the wards for yourself, he invited. "It's not a big problem compared to the number of people with alcohol-induced hallucinosis, who are psychotic with the DTs [delirium tremens], suicidal when drunk. It is nothing compared to the effect of alcohol on your mental health."

There was a big gap between the hopeless grey mood of the midweek comedown, the Ecstasy hangover that most clubbers learned how to deal with, and Dr John Henry's bleak prediction that Ecstasy might create a future generation of manic depressives. Once again, tangible facts were hard to come by.

CHAPTER TWO

Club Drugs Since the Late 1990s

Ketamine Is Becoming a Popular Club Drug

John Cloud

Ketamine is an anesthetic that was first administered to American soldiers during the Vietnam War. It is rarely used on human patients these days because of the disorienting and unpleasant side effects it produces, but veterinarians continue to use it to anesthetize small animals such as cats and rabbits. Ketamine, or "Special K," has also been used as a recreational drug since the 1970s, but it was not until the late 1990s that its popularity skyrocketed, as John Cloud describes in this selection. In 1997 teenagers began to take ketamine at raves in suburbs around the country. Cloud also discusses the physical effects of ketamine, which include a blocking of sensory input. Users enter a dissociative state in which they lose their sense of identity and awareness of the outside world while still remaining conscious. When Cloud's article was published in 1997 legislators were pushing to impose stronger restrictions on the drug. In 1999 ketamine became a Schedule III drug, making it illegal to possess without a license or prescription. Cloud is a reporter for *Time* magazine.

It's 5:30 on a Sunday morning, but the 400-plus kids at the Fantasy Ranch dance club won't be making it to church. Instead, amid sweeping lights and the raw thumps of the aptly named song "Insomnia," they sing the praises of the most recent drug to hit central Florida: Special K. "It's the bomb," gushes Tom, a sweaty 15-year-old with a struggling goatee. "It

will make you like this," he says, rolling his eyes up as if staring at his brain. "It's dreamy. You see the lights, like, bend."
   Tom's friend Sara quickly pulls a glass vial from her bra. After a glance around for security, she holds the black-capped vial under a pulsing light, revealing the powder she first came across in July [1997]. Now, she says, "I'm into it like every weekend." Sara is 16, and what she's into is an anesthetic sometimes administered to people but, more commonly, to cats and monkeys. Generically called ketamine, street K is most often diverted in liquid form from vets' offices or medical suppliers. Dealers dry the liquid (usually by cooking it) and grind the residue into powder. K causes hallucinations because it blocks chemical messengers in the brain that carry sensory input; the brain fills the resulting void with visions, dreams, memories, whatever. Sara says that once, after snorting several "bumps" of K, she thought other kids on the dance floor had been decapitated. "But I mean, I really knew they had heads. I was just, like, 'This is so weird.'"
   And, apparently, enticing. After 25 years of underground recreational use by big-city clubgoers and New Age types ([psychologist and drug advocate] Timothy Leary was, of course, a fan), K has exploded in the past few months onto the suburban drug scene. In February [1997], the U.S. Drug Enforcement Administration warned that use is increasing at teen "rave" parties, the marathon dances that have spawned a new youth subculture. Anti-drug czar Barry McCaffrey's office added K to its list of "emerging drugs" in 1995; the office's latest "pulse check" of the nation found K "all over." St. Louis, Mo., Tampa, Fla., and suburban New Jersey have seen a rash of animal-hospital break-ins by thieves hunting for ketamine.
   The surest sign of K's popularity, however, is that it is seeping into pop culture: In an *X-Files* [TV] episode earlier this year [1997], [FBI] agent Fox Mulder had a rogue doctor dose him with ketamine in an attempt to recover memories. The Chemical Brothers, an electronic-music group, recorded a song called "Lost in the K-Hole" for their most recent album, which went

gold last month. "K-hole" is jargon for a bad trip—too much K causes massive sensory deprivation, immobilizing and detaching a user from reality. This is not your father's groovy toke. London researcher Karl Jansen says the drug even reproduces the brain's chemical reaction to a "near-death experience."

All this attention has alarmed people like Lieutenant Bill Queen, who works narcotics in the Pinellas County sheriff's office, near Tampa Bay. He had never heard of K before December [1996]. Now, his undercover officers can buy it every week. "These kids don't know what they're getting into," says Queen. "But I can tell you, this is another drug that's going to be abused and cause harm." What really steams officer Queen is that he can't do much about it. Snorting K may be foolish, but it's not a felony. If someone without a medical or veterinary license is caught with ketamine in Florida, the maximum sentence is 60 days in jail and a $500 fine. Only a handful of state's attorneys have taken the time to prosecute K cases when the stakes are so tiny. For his part, Queen hasn't arrested anyone with K. "We could," he says, "but we're waiting," gathering evidence against dealers who sell it to his undercover cops. Next year, the legislature will consider a bill to "schedule" ketamine as a controlled substance, which would stiffen penalties. [Ketamine was scheduled in Florida in 1998.]

A swift and simple solution, right? Well, no. Outlawing drugs like LSD (in the 1960s) and Ecstasy (in the 1980s) was easy since they have no government-acknowledged medical use and aren't made by licensed firms. But ketamine and other drugs that are actually medicines are different. Senator Joseph Biden discovered how delicate drug politics can be last year [1996] when he designed a bill to control ketamine and the so-called date-rape drug Rohypnol more closely. At the time, rapists' use of the latter to sedate victims had sparked an outcry, but the Rohypnol-controlling part of the legislation died under pharmaceutical-industry pressure. The industry, whose political action committees last year donated $2.1 million to Republican candidates and $714,000 to Democrats, doesn't want the added administrative burdens and federal oversight that come with scheduling a drug as a controlled substance. (Rohypnol was already scheduled, but the bill would have regulated it further.) Each unit of a scheduled drug must be scrupulously accounted for, and some doctors won't prescribe drugs stigmatized by that heavy designation. In the case of ketamine, neither Parke-Davis, which developed the drug, nor Fort Dodge Laboratories, which makes the veterinary brand Ketaset, opposes tighter restrictions. But the industry's supporters in Congress are loath to change industry-friendly precedent, which allows drugs to be scheduled only after lengthy administrative review. (States are more willing to flout industry wishes. So far, eight have added the drug to their books.) [In 1999, ketamine became a Schedule III drug in the United States, illegal to possess without a license or prescription.]

Lost in these political battles is a basic question: is ketamine really dangerous? Maybe not. The British government decided not to closely restrict ketamine because it could not prove that K's effects were severe. Most drug-overdose deaths result from circulatory or respiratory failure, and ketamine doesn't usually depress these functions. Dr. Alex Stalcup, medical director of a California drug-treatment center, says the effects of K are "basically like being really, really drunk. It's really not a demon, not compared with the other stuff we're seeing with kids now," including smokable versions of heroin and speed.

Still, the possibility of K-high youths getting behind the wheel of a car is alarming, and ketamine was used in several rapes in the 1980s. Stalcup and others agree that ketamine can be addictive. "Some people get very habituated," says Ann Shulgin, a longtime drug researcher. "I've heard some uncomfortable stories—highly intelligent people who just don't seem aware that they're getting into a dependency."

A prominent experimenter with ketamine was John Lilly, a neuroscientist who pioneered communication with dolphins, and who was played by William Hurt in *Altered States* (1980).

Lilly recalls that a doctor first gave him ketamine in the '70s for migraines. Lilly then began injecting himself with K and at one point was taking 50 milligrams an hour, 20 hours a day, for three weeks. He became convinced "that he was a visitor from the year 3001" and that he was talking to aliens. Today, Lilly is 82 and lives in Maui. He says he hasn't done K for "about a year" and believes it's not addictive. "Go out and try some," he urges. But he also says ketamine should be illegal. "It's dangerous if you don't know what you're doing," he says. "You could fall down."

Back at the Fantasy Ranch in Tampa, the kids have never heard of John Lilly or his friend Timothy Leary. "No, man, are they dealers?" asks one. When the deejay spins a song called "A Little Bit of Ecstasy," cheers go up. "K is really fun," says Beth, 19, as she sashays away. "But I always know I'll be tired the next day."

Users Underestimate the Deadly Risks of GHB

Tamar Nordenberg

The club drug GHB (gamma hydroxybutyrate) is a slightly bitter liquid that in small doses produces feelings of euphoria but in high doses can cause unconsciousness and even coma. In the 1980s, before its dangers were known, GHB was sold in health food stores as a sleep aid and as a supplement for bodybuilders. However, in 1990 the Food and Drug Administration banned GHB after it was discovered to cause side effects ranging from nausea to seizures and coma. In 2000 President Bill Clinton signed legislation making it a federal offense to possess the drug, which had been used to facilitate date rapes. Nonetheless, many young people have continued to experiment with GHB. In this selection Tamar Nordenberg tells the story of a young man who suffered a fatal GHB overdose after mistaking the colorless, odorless drug for water. The dead man's parents subsequently founded Project GHB, Inc., a nonprofit corporation dedicated to educating the public about the dangers of recreational drugs. Nordenberg is a staff writer for *FDA Consumer Magazine* and the author of numerous health and medical articles.

Caleb will sleep deeply for awhile, but then wake up and carry on. Just check on him every so often to make sure he's positioned on his

Tamar Nordenberg, "The Death of the Party," *FDA Consumer Magazine*, vol. 34, March/April 2000.

side and still breathing, but don't bother calling 911 and incurring that huge expense for nothing.

That, says Caleb Shortridge's stepmother, Anya, is what friends advised Shortridge's roommate, Sarah, on April 30, 1998. On that hot San Diego day, the thirsty Shortridge had taken a few chugs from a water bottle his friend had set on the coffee table before realizing that the clear liquid was not water, but GHB, or gamma hydroxybutyrate, says Anya. But, she adds, Shortridge and his friends weren't overly concerned about the amount he drank of the euphoria-producing "party drug."

Shortridge was familiar with the drug, she explains, from the all-night "rave" dance parties that he and his friends frequented and where he sometimes performed as a disc jockey. In fact, she adds, he was the person friends would go to for advice like "Which drugs can I take safely?" and "Which shouldn't I mix together?"

So Shortridge's friends found it ironic, on top of tragic, Anya says, that he was the one who ended up dead at age 27 from a drug overdose. "It gave them all a wake-up call," she says.

Anya and Shortridge's father, Ken, now devote themselves to waking others up to the life-threatening dangers of the drug that took their son's life. Last Dec. 3 [1999], they appeared on a *"Leeza"* talk show segment on *Sex, Drugs, and Death*, sharing the stage with other families whose loved ones were killed by party drugs.

Not as Harmless as Users Think

Try as she might to alert people to GHB's dangers, Anya says, some people inevitably won't hear the message until something terrible happens to them. "It's naive people that are getting hurt," she says. "We get letters saying, 'You don't know what you're talking about. If he had done this properly . . . If there was this circumstance . . . If you know what you're doing, this won't happen to you.'"

But if you really do know what you're doing, experts say,

you know that anyone can accidentally overdose on GHB, also known on the street as *salty water, scoop, GBH, grievous bodily harm, Georgia home boy, liquid ecstasy, liquid x, somatomax, goop,* or simply *G.*

By powerfully and rapidly depressing the central nervous system, GHB can produce an intoxicated feeling that has earned it a reputation as a pleasure enhancer for thrill-seeking youngsters. But its side effects can range from nausea and vomiting to delusions, depression, vertigo, hallucinations, seizures, difficulty breathing, slowed heart rate, low blood pressure, amnesia, and coma.

The U.S. Drug Enforcement Administration officially cites more than 45 deaths and 5,500 emergency room overdoses associated with GHB. Since 1990, the Food and Drug Administration [FDA] has issued multiple warnings to consumers about the drug's sometimes-deadly effects.

A Clear Threat

GHB was first synthesized in 1960 and, before its harmful potential became known, was sold at health food stores as a dietary supplement. In the '80s, GHB was popular among bodybuilders because of its supposed ability to release a growth hormone and stimulate muscle growth.

But in 1990, based on more than 30 reports of GHB-linked illness, the FDA declared the product unsafe and illegal except in the carefully controlled environment of agency-approved drug studies. Still today, however, GHB continues to be illegally promoted, not just for inducing an uninhibited high and for building muscles, but also for combating depression, aiding sleep, and fostering weight loss. . . .

[In 1999], in response to renewed abuse of the drug, the FDA reissued its warning, telling consumers again about GHB's risks and reiterating that the drug has never been approved for sale as a medical product in the United States.

The FDA has also warned consumers about two potentially

deadly "chemical cousins" of GHB, which are precursors of the drug that are converted into GHB in the body:

• **gamma butyrolactone, or GBL,** which is marketed under brand names such as *Renewtrient, Revivarant* or *Revivarant G, Blue-Nitro* or *Blue Nitro Vitality, GH Revitalizer, Gamma G,* and *Remforce.*

• **1,4 butanediol, abbreviated BD,** a chemical in products sold under brand names like *Revitalize Plus, Serenity, Enliven, GHRE, SomatoPro, NRG3, Thunder Nectar,* and *Weight Belt Cleaner.*

Reports Underestimate the Problem

Nationwide, the government's Drug Abuse Warning Network has tracked an increase in GHB-related emergency room visits from 20 in 1992 to more than 750 in 1997. But these statistics are the "tip of the iceberg," warns rave drug specialist and former narcotics detective Trinka Porrata, who adds, "Kids are dropping like flies."

Two things help explain why official reports under-represent the problem by far, Porrata says: Emergency rooms often can't detect or identify the drug because it leaves the body in about 12 hours, and many doctors are not yet familiar with this relatively new drug of abuse.

Despite the bleak statistics, young people are freely experimenting with GHB. Cities reporting widespread use include Boston, Honolulu, Los Angeles, Baltimore, Detroit, Phoenix, Miami, New York, Atlanta, Minneapolis/St. Paul, Dallas, Seattle, San Francisco, San Diego, New Orleans, and Newark, according to the National Institute on Drug Abuse.

How They Take It

Around Florida State University, says 20-year-old junior Debbie Mallard (not her real name), GHB is "very popular. At clubs, they go around and sell it to you in a shot." One of Mallard's friends uses it as an alternative to drinking when she goes out because she doesn't like the taste of alcohol. "With

GHB, you can get the same effect [as alcohol] with such a small amount," says Mallard. And compared to other drugs, GHB is cheap—$5 to $10 for a capful or teaspoonful dose, according to the Office of National Drug Control Policy.

Usually made as a clear liquid or a light-colored powder that the user mixes with water, alcohol or soda, GHB's identity is easily masked. At night clubs and raves, partiers often carry the drug around in Visine [eye drop] bottles or simple water bottles like the one from which Shortridge drank the day he died. The drug hasn't been dubbed *salty water* for nothing. Anya says, "It looks just like water. It's scary."

Scary, because people can accidentally drink it like Shortridge did, or be tricked into drinking it when someone secretly laces their drink with the so-called "date-rape drug.". . .

For those who take GHB deliberately, the objective is to hit the "right level," says Porrata, "where you get the out-of-body buzz, like you're watching yourself on T.V." But, she says, it's a goal that many overshoot, risking deadly overdose.

Kids think passing out is just a part of doing G, Porrata says. Student Mallard agrees: "When you're in college, you don't think anything's going to happen to you. I've seen people pass out. People are always falling down at clubs, but you're in your own world and you don't really care. You think, 'Oh, that's a bummer.'"

When GHB Turns Deadly

And what about when someone dies from a condition called pulmonary edema, the symptoms of which Porrata describes as "blood frothing out of their nose and mouth all over the place?" Well, then they rationalize that the person just took too much, says the ex-detective.

"They all think they'll be more careful, but you can't be careful about a drug like this with no predictability," Porrata says. "The dose that might make a 150-pound girl high could kill a 300-pound man. And the dose that made you high yesterday might kill you today." The fact that the drug is made in clandestine laboratories—often in people's homes—compounds its unpredictability, according to the Drug Enforcement Administration.

GHB is especially dangerous when mixed with alcohol or, as Mallard reports is common at her school, taken with ecstasy or other drugs. But contrary to common misrepresentations on the Internet, GHB also often kills or injures all by itself.

Controlling GHB Use

To curb GHB production, the FDA's Office of Criminal Investigations has participated in numerous investigations and prosecutions related to the drug's illegal manufacture and distribution. . . . [As of early 2000], the government has won more than 33 GHB-related convictions. . . .

Based on its abuse potential, [in early 2000], Congress was considering GHB for "scheduling" under the Controlled Substances Act. If GHB is classified as a controlled substance, the act would set forth federal penalties, including imprisonment and fines, for marketing the drug illegally. [GHB was categorized as a Schedule I drug in March 2000.]

In addition to the extent of a drug's abuse potential, the decision whether to schedule a drug and how strictly to control it depends on factors such as:

• The drug's capacity for producing physical and psychological dependence. GHB has been shown to cause addiction with sustained use. Withdrawal symptoms can include insomnia, muscle cramps, tremor, and anxiety.

• Whether the drug has an accepted medical use. [By 2000], GHB was not approved for any use in the United States but was being studied to treat the symptoms of a sleep disorder called narcolepsy. In Europe, GHB has been used as an anesthetic and experimentally to treat alcohol withdrawal.

More than 20 states have already classified GHB as a controlled substance [as of early 2000]. And some other states impose criminal penalties for the drug's possession though they haven't scheduled it.

Public Education

To truly fetter GHB use, however, experts emphasize that public education is needed to complement these legal actions. The National Institute on Drug Abuse is dedicating $54 million to a national campaign with partner organizations Join Together, National Families in Action, the American Academy of Child and Adolescent Psychiatry, and the Community Anti-Drug Coalitions of America to alert teens, young adults, parents, educators, and others to the dangers of GHB and other club drugs.

Porrata, Anya Shortridge, and others hope that such legitimate public education will outweigh the often inaccurate information disseminated by individuals over the Internet. Internet authors who enjoy taking illegal drugs are not to be counted on for correct, unbiased information, Porrata points out.

As for the common Internet claim that a person who passes out from GHB will wake up in four hours, don't count on it. Anya pleads on her own Website [www.projectghb.org], "If anyone you know has used GHB or any other substance and has passed out and is unarousable and/or having seizures: *Call 911 immediately!*"

Porrata offers this additional advice: Since even those who are near death from GHB use typically don't remember the experience, videotaping people when they're exhibiting dangerous symptoms may help convince them of the problem's seriousness.

Don't yet know of anyone who's been harmed by the so-called party drug? Count yourself lucky, says Janet Woodcock, M.D., director of the FDA's Center for Drug Evaluation and Research. "Like many dangerous habits, sometimes you can get away with it for a while. But then your number may come up."

The Club Drug Scene Is Growing More Dangerous

Sara Trollinger

Drug use among teens at the beginning of the twenty-first century is more serious than in the 1960s, according to author Sara Trollinger. In this selection she argues that young people are taking drugs at earlier ages and progressing faster to harder drugs, such as MDMA. Today's club drugs are easy to hide inside candy or eye drop bottles, places usually overlooked during drug checks. However, the consequences of using drugs remain grave: clouded minds, fatal overdoses, and drug-facilitated sexual assaults. Trollinger is founder and president of the House of Hope, a Christian-sponsored group home for troubled teens, in Orlando, Florida. Trollinger has taught in the Orange County (Florida) Juvenile Detention Center as well as in public schools. A noted speaker on youth issues, she has frequently addressed the U.S. Congress.

The kids at House of Hope [a Christian teen home in Orlando, Florida] love Detective Scott Perkins. He had been an undercover cop with the Orlando Police Department until he got shot up during a successful hostage rescue a couple of years ago.

I first saw Scott on an Orlando TV program being interviewed about his work. "Parents don't have a clue that their kids are bringing disguised drugs into their homes," said Scott, and I nodded my head in agreement. I knew right away that I had to get in touch with this streetwise cop and bring him to the House of Hope to educate our staff and talk to the teens about the dangers of going back on drugs.

We immediately liked Scott, a friendly, outgoing, and approachable fellow in his mid-thirties. As he regaled us with stories from his undercover days, we soon realized that he is a brave guy who has stayed alive by employing his street-savvy wits. Our kids recognize courage when they see it. I've asked Scott to be my expert on the teen drug scene because he worked undercover for six years—a long time in that dangerous line of work.

Scott certainly has a way of grabbing the kids' attention. All it takes is for him to start telling a few stories about taking down the bad guys, and our House of Hope kids want to hear more. Throughout much of the 1990s, Scott's job was to infiltrate Orlando's burgeoning rave scene and discover who the drug dealers were. He witnessed their handiwork every weekend at the raves. "I saw it all," he says. "Kids experiencing seizures and blackouts. Kids uncontrollable due to the various 'designer' and 'club' drugs they were ingesting at rave parties. One time I saw a kid shuffle out of the warehouse, drop to the ground, and start flopping like a fish," said Scott. "Then he vomited and spit up foam. It was bad, man."

Scott speaks in a matter-of-fact manner of someone who's seen too many drug overdoses, or "ODs," over the years. He's been in too many Orlando hospital emergency rooms, trying to comfort inconsolable parents who had been asked to identify their dead son or daughter. . . .

Kids Are Easy Pickings

Raves began as nirvana-like parties in which the zonked-out participants promoted peace, love, unity, and respect. Organized drug dealers have found raves to be easy pickings to sell heroin, GHB, crystal-meth, and other deadly drugs. . . . The effects of drugs *enhance* the intensity of the music and lights. If someone comes along and says that ecstasy or GHB is the ticket to ride, who's going to say no in such a free-for-all, chaotic atmosphere? . . .

The Changes in Drug Use Patterns

In many respects, there's nothing new under the sun regarding teenage drug use. What's happening is that kids are being introduced to many different things at a much earlier age than they used to be. . . . [Once] there was a rather orderly progression: teens smoked cigarettes, discovered beer, and moved on to Jack Daniel's [whiskey]. Then they started smoking pot, which was an entryway to acid. For most teens back in the sixties and seventies, this is where their drug use leveled out.

Today's teens still follow the progressive route, although they are prone to skip over several steps. They may start smoking in grade school before ditching the Marlboros for a cigarette with some punch—marijuana. Once that loses its thrill, it's time to experiment with pills such as [sedatives] Valium and Seconol. Then their drug use becomes *serious*. They turn their attention to several new "designer" drugs, the most popular being MDMA (methylene dioxymethamphetamine), otherwise known as XTC or "ecstasy." Painted like candy canes or imprinted with Nike swooshes to appeal to adolescents, ecstasy pills are sold on the street for prices ranging from $15 to $25.

"Ecstasy combines the energy that amphetamines give you with the slight hallucinations of LSD," explained Detective Scott. "Plus, ecstasy has components that break down communication barriers, which is why it has been so popular in raves. Ecstasy causes you to ignore the body's warning signals that it needs rest and water. You can literally dance yourself into a heat stroke. If you combine ecstasy with alcohol, which is a diuretic, your body becomes drained of fluids much more quickly. I saw ravers just dance themselves into exhaustion."

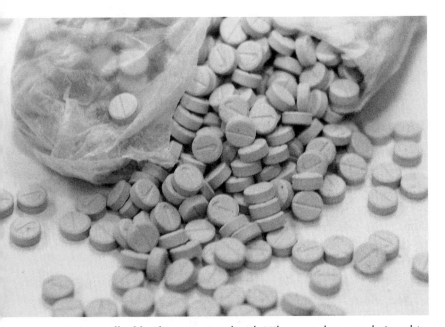

Ecstasy pills, like these imprinted with Nike swooshes, are designed to appeal to adolescents.

Ecstasy comes in various pill forms called "Lightning Bolts," "Doves," "Smurfs," "Bootlegs," "Blue Pandas," and "Pink Triangles." These pills, about the size of aspirin, can be ingested orally, but you don't feel anything for about half an hour. Many kids snort ecstasy in a powder form so they can get high within five to ten minutes.

And what a high. Users experience an abundance of energy and a desire for touching and hugging. Body massages intensify the high, as does sexual behavior. Kids on ecstasy are said to be "rolling," "peaking," "blowing up," or "X-ing." One of the involuntary side effects of ecstasy, however, is teeth grinding and biting the lips and tongue.

The Users Speak

Smoking weed and doing acid was boring. I didn't like it. Then one of my friends showed me ecstasy and said I would love it, that it would feel as though my skin was flying off. Ecstasy sounded like fun, so I took it. Most kids have a drug of choice. My drug of choice became ecstasy.

—*Kelli*, age fifteen

I can tell you why kids take more and more drugs. It goes like this: if speed and crack take you up to the fourth floor, then why not go all the way to the twelfth floor and take a chance with harder drugs? Either way, the fall will kill you.

—*Curtis*, age sixteen . . .

Today's Paraphernalia

[As Detective Scott describes]:

When I speak before parents, I pull out a backpack and start taking items out of it. "Everything that is coming out of this pack is drugs or drug paraphernalia," I say. Of course, most parents are thinking about rolling papers, roach clips, and bongs—stuff from the seventies. Not any more these days. The first thing I pull out is an M&M bag. The second thing is a Skittles bag. The next is a Tootsie Roll bag. The fourth is a Blow Pop bag. The fifth is a pacifier. Then I reach down and pull out glow sticks, a Vicks inhaler, a surgical mask, a heavy-duty balloon, a condom, a string, a rubber band, a stick of gum, a Visine [eye drop] bottle, a bottle of water, and a bottle of bubbles. Each one of these items has a very specific function for drug users.

Those using ecstasy suck on a Blow Pop candy or pacifier because the drug makes you grind your teeth and bite your tongue. The M&M and Skittles bags contain ecstasy "rolls" or pills. Kids take a bag of M&Ms, use a knife to cut open a slit, and then dump out the chocolate candies. The candy bag is then refilled with ecstasy pills, which have the same feel as the chocolate candy. They tape up the bag and lay it right on the table in front of everybody's face.

The Tootsie Rolls are the smaller, individually wrapped ones you normally purchase in fifty- or one hundred-packs. The kids go outside and place a few on the sidewalk to let the sun melt them a bit. Then they bring them inside, unwrap them, put an ecstasy tablet inside and rewrap them. The kids do that so they won't get busted. If an undercover cop sees them handing a Tootsie Roll to someone, he probably won't interfere.

The same thing happens with a stick of gum. Dealers unwrap the gum, give it a small hit of acid, and wrap it up again. A kid with a fifty-pack of gum spiked with LSD can walk around school all day with this gum in his backpack. If you asked any cop when the last time was that he searched a piece of gum, he would reply, "Never!"

The Visine bottle, used primarily by sexual predators, is filled with a drug called GHB. They arrive at a rave, notice an attractive girl, strike up a conversation, and when she's not looking, squeeze a couple of drops of GHB into her drink.

GHB works in three stages. In the first stage, she feels sexually aggressive and comes on to a guy. The second stage is when she says she doesn't feel good. The third stage is when she passes out. The guy who doses her knows all the stages. As soon as she complains about not feeling good, he suggests taking her outside for some "fresh air." By the time they get outside, he's got her. She's done for. I tell you, it's a crazy world, man.

The Hazards of GHB

According to Scott, GHB used to be sold in health food stores as a form of growth hormone stimulant or a sleep disorder medicine. It was taken off the shelves in 1991 when the Food and Drug Administration learned that GHB was being used by kids to get high. Scott says GHB is easy to produce; most GHB is produced in home labs or bathtubs, sometimes by kids ordering GHB kits off the Internet. They mix some nasty-sounding ingredients (engine degreaser, muratic acid, Drano, and some vinegar), and voila!—they produce a clear, odorless liquid that contains a salty taste.

GHB gives teens a stimulated-type high, but if they drink too much, they overdose. "GHB overdoses are the most incredible scenes you'll ever see in your life," said Scott. "Kids vomit, shake, then almost stop breathing. Their heart rates practically shut down. They look like they could die at any moment. They usually stay in this form of 'blackout' for three hours. When the drug starts to wear off, we call it the 'dawn syndrome,' the time they start coming out of it."

GHB is the drug to watch out for. Its initials stand for gamma hydroxybutyrate, but "grievous harm to the body" would be closer to the truth. The drug has been linked to at least sixty deaths since 1990 and more than 5,700 recorded overdoses, according to the Drug Enforcement Administration.

Drugs and Date Rape

Sexual predators love GHB because it's the ultimate "date rape" drug. A discreet and undetected squeeze of the Visine bottle causes a girl to experience euphoria, hallucinations, followed by a deep sleep. She won't remember *anything*. That's when she can be taken advantage of—by several guys taking turns.

> I can't remember what happened that night. I woke up thirteen, fourteen hours later at a friend's house. Somebody told me I drank GHB and that what I did after that was consensual. Maybe it was; maybe it wasn't.
> —*Andrea*, age fifteen

"I've read hundreds of victim statements over the years," said Detective Scott. "The typical statement is a young woman or teen girl stating that she was hanging out at a rave or a nightclub, and then she met a guy with black hair named Johnny who asked her to dance. After the dance, he offered to buy her a drink, and the next thing she knew, she woke up under the fire escape with her clothes off and a pain in her thighs. I've also heard about instances in which a girl was at a non-alcohol establishment, drinking a Sprite, and then waking up under the same circumstances."

Sometimes young women never wake up. A fifteen-year-old girl in Detroit died after drinking a soda laced with GHB at a party. Four young men who caused her death were sentenced to prison terms ranging from five to fifteen years.

GHB has replaced rohypnol—or "roofies"—as the date-rape drug of choice. The laws against rohypnol are so severe that if you are arrested for having the drug in your possession, you're toast with the judicial system. Rohypnol and a date-rape cousin called clonazepam cause amnesia, serious motor impairment, and even respiratory failure. They're still prevalent drugs because they're cheap—usually $1 each, which is why they've earned the sobriquet "dollar date.". . .

What we've found at House of Hope is that the root problem of drug use is spiritual. If teens have a reason larger than themselves not to take drugs and to have hope in the future, they can get off the drugs.

Rohypnol and GHB Facilitate Rape

Nora Fitzgerald and K. Jack Riley

Club drugs can be used to commit more serious crimes than illegal possession. Since at least the mid-1990s, the club drugs Rohypnol and GHB have been used to facilitate sexual assault by rendering victims incapable of resistance. In this selection, Nora Fitzgerald and K. Jack Riley examine the recreational and criminal use of these drugs and the problems faced by law enforcement in investigating drug-facilitated rapes. Fitzgerald is a social science analyst at the National Institute of Justice; Riley is the associate director of infrastructure, safety, and environment for the nonprofit think tank RAND Corporation.

More than 430,000 sexual assaults occur annually in the United States, according to victimization surveys. Many of these assaults involve alcohol and drugs, which are often used voluntarily by both victim and offender. But in the mid- and late 1990's, ethnographers and rape crisis centers began hearing reports of drugs, often referred to as "roofies" and "liquid ecstasy," being administered clandestinely to immobilize victims, impair their memory, and thus facilitate rape. Two drugs in particular were mentioned in these reports: Rohypnol (the pharmaceutical trade name for flunitrazepam) and GHB (gamma-hydroxybutyrate).

These drugs can produce loss of consciousness and the inability to recall recent events. Victims may not be aware that

Nora Fitzgerald and K. Jack Riley, "Drug-Facilitated Rape: Looking for the Missing Pieces," *National Institute of Justice Journal*, April 2000, p. 8.

they have ingested drugs or that they have been raped while under the influence of drugs. Reports of such assaults and increases in the recreational consumption of the drugs used in these assaults have brought drug-facilitated rape into sharp focus in recent years.

This article summarizes findings about drug-facilitated rape learned by researchers at the U.S. Department of Justice in response to a request from the Attorney General for more information about this new phenomenon. . . .

What Are Rape-Facilitating Drugs?

Sexual assault victims who believe drugs were surreptitiously given to them typically report remembering sensations of drunkenness that do not correspond with the amounts of alcohol consumed, unexplained gaps in memory, altered levels of consciousness, and unexplainable signs of physical trauma. The most commonly implicated drugs are Rohypnol and GHB.

Rohypnol, or flunitrazepam, belongs to a class of drugs called benzodiazepines and is approved for use in 80 countries, but not in the United States or Canada. It is available only in pill form, is tasteless, odorless, and colorless, and dissolves to some degree in liquid.

Benzodiazepines are used primarily to produce sedation, sleep, or muscle relaxation; to reduce seizures and anxiety; and to produce anterograde amnesia, a desired effect for some surgical procedures. *Anterograde* amnesia is a condition in which events that occurred during the time the drug was in effect are forgotten, in contrast to *retrograde* amnesia, in which events prior to the intervening agent are forgotten.

Rohypnol mentally and physically incapacitates an individual, particularly when used in combination with alcohol, and is capable of producing anterograde amnesia.

GHB, a drug first synthesized in the 1920's, occurs naturally in the human body in minute amounts. It was under development as an anesthetic agent in the late 1950's and early

1960's, but no commercial products were developed from these efforts. Until the FDA banned the drug in 1990, it was available through health food stores and marketed as both a sleep aid and a body-building supplement. Several vendors distributed products containing GHB under trade names such as "Gamma Hydrate" and "Somatomax PM."

GHB is marketed in some European countries as an adjunct to anesthesia and currently [as of 2000] is being tested for treatment of narcolepsy as well as alcohol addiction and withdrawal (with mixed results) in Europe and the United States.

Statistics on Rohypnol

No one really knows how common drug-facilitated rape is because today's research tools do not offer a means of measuring the number of incidents. However, recent findings from ethnographic research and school-based surveys can provide insight into the voluntary use of these drugs.

Flunitrazepam first appeared in early warning ethonographic systems in December 1993, when it was reported among Miami high school students.

By 1995, the Community Epidemiology Working Group (CEWG) found that use of Rohypnol was spreading in Florida and Texas. *Pulse Check* [published by the U.S. Office of National Drug Control Policy] reported Rohypnol use was rising, particularly among youth and young adults. Ethnographers in Florida and Texas reported that local law enforcement agents were seizing more Rohypnol tablets, often still in the manufacturer's packaging.

In 1996, Monitoring the Future (MTF) began tracking Rohypnol. In 1999, MTF found that 0.5 percent of 8th graders and 1.0 percent of 10th and 12th graders had reported using Rohypnol in 1998, a level slightly below those found a year earlier. Such rates appear low in comparison to marijuana or amphetamine use, but they are not trival—10th and 12th graders report similar levels of heroin use.

In 1997, Pulse Check noted that although Rohypnol continued to be available in Florida and Texas, distribution had slowed.

In 1998, Texas' statewide student survey, which uses the same methodology and many of the same items as MTF, found that 1.3 to 2.1 percent of Texas students in grades 8 to 12 reported use of Rohypnol during the school year. Later in 1998, Pulse Check reported that Rohypnol was in use in Florida, Hawaii, Minnesota, and Texas.

Statistics on GHB

Mention of widespread recreational use of GHB only recently has been reported by CEWG in December 1997. In winter 1998, Pulse Check reported use of GHB in many urban areas.

The Drug Abuse Warning Network (DAWN) also has captured information about GHB because of overdoses. The Drug Enforcement Administration has documented approximately 650 overdoses and 20 deaths related to GHB. MTF added questions about GHB to its year 2000 survey.

Available law enforcement statistics on seizures and trafficking (primarily from the Drug Enforcement Administration) tend to corroborate the ethnographic and survey data.

Ethnographic measures may not represent the true scale of the drugs' use, however, and more rigorous scientific measures have not been in place long enough to give researchers the ability to project accurate trends.

Problems Collecting Drug-Rape Statistics

Another factor complicating science's ability to measure the incidence and prevalence of these drugs is the lack of law enforcement evidence. Investigations of suspected drug-facilitated assaults often turn out to be inconclusive because many victims do not seek assistance until hours or days later, in part because the drugs have impaired recall and in part because victims may not recognize the signs of sexual assault. By the time they do report a suspected assault, conclusive forensic evidence may have been lost. Even when victims do suspect a drug-facilitated rape and seek help immediately, law enforcement agencies may not know how to collect evidence appropriately or how to test urine using the sensitive method required. . . .

To add more complexity to the puzzle, school-based surveys seem to suggest that Rohypnol and GHB are consumed voluntarily, perhaps increasingly so, because these drugs are cheap, easy to share, and easy to hide. Use appears to be concentrated among populations that also are at the highest risk

 THE HISTORY OF DRUGS

The Physical Effects of GHB

The club drug GHB acts as a sedative and can easily be used to render a victim incapable of resisting sexual assault.

GHB appears to be the latest in the constantly changing and trendy club and party drug scene. GHB, like many other drugs du jour, has been around for a long time—it was developed in the 1980s as a surgical anesthetic, but then it became popular as a muscle-building and weight-loss potion.

When combined with alcohol, GHB acts like a sedative and has had the effect on potential rape victims of causing unconsciousness, memory loss, and persistent tiredness. The sometimes unpredictable effects of GHB, along with its potential to cause vertigo, reduced heart rate, seizures, respiratory failure, and even coma, prompted the government to ban its use and sale, except for licensed research. GHB is commonly used with other drugs, including X (Ecstasy). Such use clouds both certainty about GHB's effects, and whether serious incidents associated with GHB were caused by that drug, or its combination with other substances. GHB seems to be particularly dangerous when mixed with alcohol.

Scott Lindquist, "Alcohol and Drugs: The Rape Enablers," *The Date Rape Prevention Book: The Essential Guide for Girls and Women*. Naperville, IL: Sourcebooks, 2000.

of sexual assault, including middle school, high school, and college-age students.

The good news is that public awareness about the drugs and their effects appears to be increasing.

What Is Being Done to Reduce Drug-Facilitated Rape?

Although current measuring methods do not reveal exactly how widespread drug-facilitated rape is, research does make it clear that the risk is real.

Since reports of drug-facilitated rape first started appearing, policy-makers at the Federal level have moved to address the situation. One step was to improve enforcement at the U.S.-Mexican border of the ban on importation of flunitrazepam. Then in October 1996, President Clinton signed the Drug-Induced Rape Prevention and Punishment Act, which provides harsh penalties for distribution or possession of flunitrazepam. In February 2000, the President [George W. Bush] signed similar legislation related to GHB.

The Office for Victims of Crime (OVC) within the Department of Justice currently is providing training and technical assistance for a model program designed to promote promising practices in sexual assault medical evidentiary exams. The program, which promotes the use of specially trained sexual assault nurse examiners, has developed a guide that addresses the issues of drug-facilitated rape, with specific information and guidance regarding comprehensive drug testing and an exam protocol.

National and local victim service organizations have responded to the situation by developing campaigns to raise awareness. A Los Angeles County task force developed a rape kit and procedures designed to improve the way evidence is gathered in suspected cases of drug-facilitated rape. The task force members included the Rape Treatment Center at Santa Monica–UCLA Medical Center, the Los Angeles County District Attorney's Office, the Los Angeles Police Department, and the

County of Los Angeles Sheriff's Department crime labs. . . .

Only four substantial studies of the prevalence and incidence of drug-facilitated rape were under way in late 1999 when this article was prepared, but none will provide an accurate measure of the situation. Three do not interview victims and therefore cannot factor in recreational use of Rohypnol or GHB. The fourth, a study by the University of Cincinnati and funded by NIJ [the National Institute of Justice], asks victims specifically if someone has ever placed Rohypnol in a beverage but does not link the responses to sexual assault victimizations or recreational use.

To understand more about drug-facilitated rape, a research agenda should include the following:

• Expansion of existing Federal data systems to provide information on drug-facilitated rape. The *National Crime Victimization Survey* may be an appropriate means for collecting population-based information on the incidence of this offense.

• Collection of new data in the fields of pharmacology and offender profiling.

• Ethnographic studies to develop a better understanding of the nature of this offense, including the most likely victims and the risk factors for victimization.

• A major multiyear, multimethod research initiative structured as four separate studies designed to measure the incidence of drug-facilitated rape among suspected cases, within the general population, among high-risk populations, and in the context of acquaintance rape.

• Funding for development of new drug detection technologies, such as hair analysis methods.

Some of the ethnographic and newspaper reporting on Rohypnol and GHB, which the Department of Justice working group tracked, has been driven in part by sporadic signs of increased recreational use and overdoses. But the more important impetus for further study appears to be reports from people who turn to rape counseling centers and clinics with complaints and suspicions that they have been victimized.

Ecstasy Is Becoming a Dangerous Street Drug

Benjamin Wallace-Wells

Ecstasy is no longer only being used at nonviolent suburban raves, writes Benjamin Wallace-Wells in this selection. The market for Ecstasy has expanded as drug dealers on the streets have begun to sell MDMA alongside crack and heroin. Some dealers also cut the physically nonaddictive Ecstasy with these highly addictive drugs in order to get young people hooked. As a result of these trends, U.S. lawmakers are working to greatly increase the penalties and jail sentences for the possession and sale of even small amounts of Ecstasy. In addition, undercover agents are focusing on cracking down on Ecstasy users at raves. Wallace-Wells argues that mandating high penalties for nonviolent Ecstasy users will uselessly crowd prisons. Instead, severe penalties should be reserved for the high-volume Ecstasy traffickers and violent street dealers, he writes. Wallace-Wells is an editor for the *Washington Monthly* and a former reporter for the *Philadelphia Inquirer*.

Until two years ago [2001], Tom Lowe's job was about as easy and worry-free as an undercover cop's can get. Lowe, the lead Ecstasy investigator for the Pennsylvania attorney general, spent most of his professional time going to raves—vast dance parties held in abandoned warehouses or clubs and fueled by

Ecstasy and electronic music. The dealers he busted, like the parties' patrons, were mostly peaceable white suburban kids, too trusting and naive to think that a cop could have even found a rave. They sold Ecstasy to him eagerly, and often without suspicion, and then he arrested them. Kids like this, more interested in partying with their friends than vetting buyers, were pretty easy pickings for Lowe, who'd cut his teeth making cocaine buys in Detroit. The hardest part of his job, he told me, had been changing the way he dressed to keep up with the latest raver trends, and making sure he knew enough about current electronic music to pass for an earnest, older raver.

But Lowe's job has gotten harder, and the raver act he'd become so good at doesn't play so well anymore. In recent years, the Ecstasy market has expanded beyond the rave scene, and more sophisticated and dangerous drug organizations have begun to elbow in on what had been mostly a friend-to-friend, white suburban trade. . . . [In 2002], Lowe put some gun-toting Latin Kings gang members in jail for Ecstasy distribution in York, Pa., after a long and difficult investigation. The drug, for Lowe, has left the trusting insularity of the rave scene and begun to move out onto the streets, where dealers are more violent, more profit-conscious, and far more wary about undercover buyers like Tom Lowe. "It's a whole new ballgame," he says. "It's not just white suburban ravers anymore."

The trends Lowe has seen in warehouses and parking lots around suburban Pennsylvania have begun to emerge nationally. The market for Ecstasy has begun to expand from those ravers into a broader user demographic—one that is both older and younger, more racially diverse, and includes people who do their drugs not at big raves but home alone. No longer a niche drug, Ecstasy has begun to attract organized, professional drug gangs. In some cities, the drug is sold on the street alongside crack and heroin, by dealers who thrive on the repeat business afforded by addicts and junkies; since Ecstasy is not itself physically addictive, they've begun cutting it with drugs that are, like methamphetamines. Ecstasy, in other words, is becoming a street drug.

"We're seeing the same things with Ecstasy that we did with cocaine in 1979," says Mark Kleiman, a professor of public policy at UCLA. The user group is expanding, prices are declining, and professional gangs are muscling in. If this new trend continues, Ecstasy may no longer be the largely self-contained, relatively low-risk diversion that it has been, but a potential gateway to addiction and violence for millions of young Americans. . . .

Physical Effects

Unlike heroin or cocaine, the drug itself is not physically addictive, though rehab centers have begun to report an increase in the number of people seeking treatment for psychological dependence on Ecstasy. And while users of hallucinogens like acid or mushrooms sometimes have "bad trips"—a chemically induced state of acute panic—anecdotal evidence suggests that those who take Ecstasy rarely do. (Reliable numbers are extraordinarily difficult to come by, because most researchers seem to blame most Ecstasy-related bad trips on corrupted drugs, or other drugs passed off as Ecstasy.) And though long-term users seem to experience highs of declining intensity after dozens of uses, scientists who study the drug aren't sure why. In a few, extremely rare cases, and particularly when users have been dancing vigorously—a hallmark of the rave culture—Ecstasy seems to be linked to sudden heart attacks in healthy young people who do not appear otherwise disposed to heart failure. (This is also true of the widely available, over-the-counter supplement ephedrine.) [Sales of products containing ephedrine were prohibited in 2004.] In the case of Ecstasy, researchers have speculated that it somehow suppresses the body's ability to sense dramatic increases in its own temperature, leading the heart to over-pump and overheat the body; some also suspect that the deaths might be largely due to impure Ecstasy cut with amphetamines, which are known to increase users' heart rates. But ravers have adapted, learning to drink lots of fluids, which helps keep their body temperatures down—go to any rave today, and you'll see hundreds of teenagers dancing with bottles of water in one hand.

Then, too, each drug is its own best and worst advertisement, and Ecstasy sells itself pretty well. In the '70s, when crystal meth first popped up on the streets of San Francisco, everybody knew pretty quickly that this was dangerous stuff: there were all these bikers running around freaked out, prone to violence, and too hopped up to function normally. Similarly, the crack epidemic died down in the mid-'90s, police and drug policy analysts think, in large part because young people growing up in crack-ridden neighborhoods saw how devastating and unshakeable that drug could be. Like marijuana, Ecstasy's a much better advertisement for itself. For the most part, chronic users seem functional—they hold down jobs and stay in touch with family and friends.

What's still not clear, however, is the effects Ecstasy has over the long term. Scientists are undecided on whether chronic use causes permanent brain damage—and will probably remain so, since the drug has only been used recreationally for about 20 years, too brief a span for any meaningful long-term studies of lifetime users. "There's a very good chance that Ecstasy may turn out to be very harmless, something like marijuana, and I'm confident that it's not as dangerous to use as cocaine and heroin," Patrick Murphy, a professor of public policy and a drug policy researcher at the University of San Francisco, told me. "But there exists the possibility that chronic use could make people very, very depressed." What we don't know about long-term Ecstasy effects alone militates against outright legalization of the drug. But as it turns out, a determined, across-the-board effort to crack down on everyone who uses it might not be much better.

Down the Drug Supply Chain

Last spring [2002], plainclothes detectives from a joint state and local force swarmed onto a foggy Camden, N.J., dock and

pried open an orange metal cargo container that was supposed to hold fresh fruit. They found what they expected—
about $3 million worth of cocaine and heroin and a couple of
dozen automatic weapons—and arrested the gang members
for whom the cargo was intended. But there was something
else in there, stuffed alongside the powdered drugs: thousands
of Ecstasy pills. "The Ecstasy was a surprise," said a spokesman for the Camden County District Attorney's Office.

It was a surprise because they hadn't thought that these sophisticated gangs were dealing Ecstasy. But it made sense. During the past two years, in parking lots along the Black Horse and
White Horse Pikes—seamy commercial strips in South Jersey—
they'd been picking up street dealers with Ecstasy as well as
their traditional products, cocaine and heroin. Ecstasy, they realized, was inching its way down the supply chain for hardcore
drugs. By the time the Office of National Drug Control Policy
[ONDCP] put out its monthly *Pulse Check* report [in] November
[2002], the trend—a more diverse user population, and a more
professional caste of dealers—was showing up across the nation. Ecstasy was being sold along with crack, cocaine, and
methamphetamines in Baltimore, Philadelphia, Denver, and Miami. Organized Ecstasy gangs were reported in cities as far-
flung as Portland, Maine, and El Paso, Texas.

Ecstasy, it turns out, isn't a big profit center for dealers the
way heroin and cocaine are, for the simple reason that it isn't
addictive. The reason drug distributors have started to add it
to their wares, suggests Rob MacCoun, a professor of public
policy and law at the University of California–Berkeley, is that
"they want to meet the diverse needs of their market"—customers ask for the drug, so the dealers feel they must provide
it or risk losing those customers to more willing competitors.
Yet when cut with amphetamines or other addictive drugs, Ecstasy becomes an ideal vehicle for hooking young people on
the harder stuff.

The geography of Ecstasy has been changing, too. In New
York, New Orleans, and Washington, D.C., reported the ONDCP,

Ecstasy was most frequently being bought in inner-city ghettos rather than suburban raves. Most ominously, its sales were moving outdoors—a leading indicator for the kind of gang violence and street-corner shootouts that have devastated so many poor neighborhoods during the crack epidemic. Once a dealer begins selling his drugs in a public place to people he doesn't know, he becomes a prime target for robbery. To protect himself, he carries a gun—and so the thieves do, too. "A street market for any expensive drug is going to be enormously disruptive to the community," Kleiman said. "This is where MDMA can get scary."

Ecstasy as a Potential Gateway Drug

So Ecstasy presents a novel dilemma. Until recently, it's been a drug that is relatively safe, popular among teenagers, and distributed mainly by non-violent amateur dealers who sell the pure, non-addictive version of the drug. But it is becoming a drug controlled by violent, professional drug traffickers, who routinely mix the drug with more dangerous, addictive—and, hence, profitable—substances, and who aim to convert today's Ecstasy users into tomorrow's crackheads, to turn Ecstasy into what it has not yet become: A gateway drug.

The challenge for policymakers, then, is to break the connection that's now being made between Ecstasy users and organized drug dealers, before it becomes a full-fledged street drug with an attendant culture of violence and addiction. And that means distinguishing between the kind of large-scale distribution that will destroy neighborhoods and lives, and the small-scale culture of social Ecstasy use and informal dealing that probably won't. Ecstasy should be illegal. But what's needed is an enforcement regime that keeps teenagers who do use it away from street gangs.

Unfortunately, current policy is trending in exactly the opposite direction. Undercover operations, for instance, now focus heavily on raves, primarily targeting users and casual dealers rather than large-scale distributors. In California, legislators introduced a bill [in 2002] that would make it harder for rave promoters to get permits, and make them civilly liable for any injury suffered by anyone high on drugs at their parties. In Congress, Sens. Joe Biden (D-Del.) and Charles Grassley (R-Iowa) crafted a bill making the promoters criminally liable for drug use in much the same way that people who own crack houses are. The bill was tabled at the end of [2002] but passed in April [2003], after being tucked into popular legislation to create an "Amber Alert" system. Meanwhile, district attorneys from Chicago to New Orleans have been prosecuting rave promoters under local laws originally passed to target owners of crack houses.

The laws are not only unfair—if someone buys a pill of Ecstasy at a bar, runs into a pole, and puts himself in a wheelchair, his parents don't get to sue the bar owner—but counterproductive. And at best, it will make buying Ecstasy at a rave no less risky than buying it on the street, from dealers looking to get them hooked on coke; at worst, the new legislation will focus law enforcement efforts disproportionately on raves, actively driving users into the arms of hardcore street dealers.

The same societally destructive incentives are increasingly being built into legal penalties for Ecstasy use and sale. The federal sentence for anyone possessing more than 8,000 Ecstasy pills now is a mandatory minimum of 10 years. This makes sense; no casual user or amateur dealer would have 8,000 pills on hand. (If you were to take a new pill each time your last high ended—which nobody does—it would take you more than five years to use up 8,000 pills.) Federal law, and most state and local laws, also mandate quite modest penalties for possession of small amounts of the drug—many states, like Delaware and Minnesota, match possession penalties for Ecstasy with those for marijuana, and allow judges to punish violators with a simple fine. This, too, makes sense. Ecstasy simply isn't as dangerous as drugs like crack. Because the uncut Ecstasy traded among ravers is not physically addictive, it's not likely to create populations of prostitutes and thieves who commit crimes to feed their habit. Nor do the drug's users die from overdosing, as users of cocaine and heroin often do. Moreover, the rapid growth of Ecstasy use has recently tapered off.

The Question of Penalties

Yet despite all this, state and local elected officials are pushing to stiffen penalties for possessing or selling small amounts of Ecstasy to bring them in line with drugs like methamphetamines, and, to a slightly lesser extent, heroin and cocaine. Simple possession in Georgia means a mandatory minimum of two years in prison. A failed 2001 bill in Illinois threatened a mandatory minimum of six years in jail for possession of 15 tablets of Ecstasy. And Texas mandates two years in jail for anyone caught with one gram of Ecstasy or more (one gram is equivalent to about four pills). Such high penalties, if they become common, will not only fill the nation's prisons with nonviolent Ecstasy users. They will also drive frightened amateur rave dealers out of business, with both positive and negative consequences. On the plus side, fewer dealers at raves should lead to less Ecstasy consumption among casual users. On the minus side, it will almost certainly drive the more determined young users toward the serious traffickers, where more addictive drugs and other dangers await.

What's needed, instead, is a two-tracked policy. Penalties and enforcement should be extremely tough on high-volume traffickers and their street-level dealers, with much lower penalties for, and less enforcement against, users and amateurs who peddle small quantities of the drug to friends and acquaintances. Instead of cracking down on raves, law enforcement should recognize that rave-based Ecstasy use will be relatively safe, especially if they tolerate the presence of testing organizations that can help ensure that users don't move on to other drugs. . . . The model here is the Dutch program of allowing users to smoke pot in licensed cannabis shops. Dutch law-makers saw that whereas cannabis use in itself was relatively benign, dangers emerged when cannabis users bought from dealers who also sold cocaine, heroin, and other hard drugs, which thrust them into a more violent drug market and exposed them to addiction. The Dutch policy has been moderately successful in keeping pot smokers away from hard drugs, according to Berkeley's MacCoun and Peter Reuter of the University of Maryland. Only 22 percent of marijuana users in Holland report having tried cocaine; 33 percent of American pot smokers say they have. (Heroin use among pot smokers in America and Holland is statistically identical.) "It's an approach which we haven't been willing to consider in America—separating the users from the real harm," MacCoun said. Raves could play a similar role for Ecstasy, containing use of the drug and keeping teenagers out of the orbit of street dealers. That wouldn't necessitate making Ecstasy legal. But it would require an attitudinal shift: Legislators and police officials would have to focus on reducing the harm caused by Ecstasy, and not simply on reducing the number of users.

Crime and Punishment

It's true, of course, that having an Ecstasy strategy that punishes low-level users and dealers far less harshly than large-scale distributors will inevitably raise charges of racism. Why should prosecutors and police let suburban white kids who do the drugs at raves and deal to their friends slide by, while cracking down harshly on criminal gangs typically led by immigrants, blacks, and Hispanics? For the simple reason that some dealers are a clear threat to the communities in which they traffic, and others are not. The sentencing disparities between cocaine and crack, for instance, are deeply unjust, putting many-fold more blacks than whites behind bars for consuming or selling what is in essence the same chemical. Yet most opponents of this injustice concede that there should be at least somewhat stiffer penalties for crack, because that form of the drug is simply more destructive to users, neighborhoods, and society generally. Moreover, a two-track penalty scheme for Ecstasy would mean relatively light treatment for all users regardless of their color. Only the big drug traffickers and their dealers would suffer.

This makes sense. I've seen this distinction while covering the Ecstasy debate: Some drug dealers carry automatic weapons, and others lose their socks. [In August 2002] I interviewed Andrew, a 17-year-old user and low-level dealer from South Jersey who'd been busted by an undercover cop. The judge in Andrew's case took pity on him and sentenced him to a rehab clinic; I met him at a coffee shop after he'd been released, last fall [2002]. He was 20 minutes late and apologized; he'd wanted to be on time but then he couldn't find clean socks. I asked him when he'd started dealing and why, and he wasn't sure. For Andrew, as for many Ecstasy users, there was a substantial gray area between using and dealing—if you give your buddy a pill, and he lets you crash at his place for a night in return and buys you dinner, are you a dealer? Andrew asked me about applying to colleges; he said he wanted to major in business. I knew someone in admissions at Dartmouth, I told him, a little helplessly. If he applied, maybe I could put in a good word. The judge had been right: Andrew clearly belonged in rehab, not in prison; he needed to be given a good primer on life, perhaps an undergraduate course catalogue, and probably a hug. Putting a guy like this in prison for five years would be deeply destructive—both to him and to society.

A Friend's Death from Ecstasy

Alexander Kogan

On July 22, 2000, a popular college student named Jamie took Ecstasy at a Manhattan dance club—his second experience with the drug. The next day he was dead. The tragedy left his friends not only heartbroken, but in a heated debate over Ecstasy. Some of Jamie's friends used club drugs and some did not. Most of the former continued to rationalize the risks even after Jamie's death. In this selection, one of Jamie's friends, writing under the pseudonym "Alexander Kogan," tells the story of the fatal night and its aftermath. The writer also reviews his own experiences and eventual disillusionment with Ecstasy, concluding that he no longer wants to rely on a drug as his source of happiness.

When I think of Jamie, the first thing that comes to mind is his body. He stood 6-foot-5 and weighed more than 300 pounds. When he wore his Oakley wraparound shades and spiked up his red hair, he looked like the biggest badass you ever saw.

Looks deceive. In the two years we were friends, I never saw Jamie get into a fight. Instead, he took that big body and did the best thing in the world with it: He hugged. He hugged the breath out of everyone he met, wrapping you in his grasp until all you could see were those thick, freckled arms and the folds of his T-shirt. You felt warm and safe, like you were wearing a suit of Jamie-armor that would protect you from harm.

That's why it hurt so much on the morning of July 23

Alexander Kogan, "The Ecstasy and the Agony: What I Learned the Hard Way from the Happy Pill," *Baltimore City Paper*, November 8, 2000. Copyright © 2000 by *Baltimore City Paper*. Reproduced by permission.

[2000], when I found out the Jamie hug I'd gotten the night before was my last.

Experimenting

We were in New York—four of my friends and I, all Johns Hopkins [University] students or recent alums—at the Manhattan dance club Twilo. We ran into some fellow Hopkins types, who mentioned that Jamie was there. I hadn't seen Jamie since the end of the semester in late May. I turned around to the main dance floor, and there was his head, poking out above a sea of people. I made a beeline for it. I got a hug.

A couple months before, we'd been lunching together in Charles Village [in the Baltimore suburbs], and I'd asked Jamie if he thought he might try ecstasy anytime soon. For a long time, Jamie was the only one in our group of club-hoppers who'd never eaten pills, but given the surge of interest in and availability of ecstasy among our peers, I figured it was only a matter of time. He told me he might, but only after he took his law-school-admission test in early June. That night at Twilo, I had to ask the all-important rave question: "Are you rolling?" Are you on ecstasy?

His answer didn't surprise me. It was his second time; the first had been only a week before. Being so big, he needed three pills to roll, but it had been "awesome." I asked him how he felt now. He raised his palms to his cheeks and gasped. "Wow."

How Ecstasy Works

This answer didn't surprise me either. Ecstasy—scientifically speaking, methylenedioxymethamphetamine or MDMA—is an amphetamine derivative that makes users feel energetic and gloriously happy. It turns up the volume on all five senses and gives you a feeling of openness and self-esteem—while rolling, I've been able to talk to the prettiest girls in a club without the fear of rejection.

Ecstasy works by manipulating the body's level of serotonin, a chemical that regulates mood, sleep, appetite, and body temperature. Generally, signals produced by the body trigger the release of serotonin; MDMA releases the serotonin without a signal, depleting almost all of the available supply—curbing appetite, raising body temperature, elevating mood, making even the slightest touch feel orgasmic. And creating tons of energy to dance the night away.

I don't remember my first time rolling very well. It was about five years ago [in the mid-1990s], when I was in high school. I remember feeling energetic, but I can't recall any particular sense of well-being or bliss. Looking back, I think that first pill wasn't really ecstasy, but a garden-variety amphetamine. In any event, the second time was different.

Becoming a Regular User

That came last January. About four months earlier, I'd gone through a messy breakup, and I spent the rest of 1999 feeling numb. I wanted something to bring me back to life. My friend Adam—who'd recently tried ecstasy and couldn't stop talking about it—invited me to a rave in Washington. I agreed; I've always liked to dance, and maybe I could meet some available cuties.

Wow.

Like Jamie, that's the only word I can think of to describe how I felt that night, and for days afterward. I spent the entire night wondering why I was smiling so much and how one little pill could make my whole outlook so different. In the days that followed, I had to keep reminding myself that it indeed was my brain—granted, with the help of a little MDMA—that had created those happy feelings. Ecstasy snapped me out of a rut; it brought me back to life, and whatever else you can say about the drug, I am thankful for that.

As the weeks progressed, I went from rolling once a month to every couple of weeks to once a week. Ecstasy gave me the perfect night every time. I could walk into a club and float. Dancing became easier, and I got better at it. I found myself meeting and talking to people I would never have had the guts to approach before.

But there was more to it than just feeling good and meeting women. Ecstasy filled a void for me. Before, my girlfriend had been the source of my happiness; now it was the pill. And there was something glamorous about feeling like I was leading two lives. By day, I was a quiet young professional clad in khakis and starched shirts. By night, I was a glitter-covered raver in orange pants, blown away on E. I felt like Dr. Jekyll and Mr. Hyde, except I loved both of my personalities, and was even finding ways to mesh the two. I think I was a kinder, warmer person at work and at home, and I was quick to talk about other aspects of my life with people at clubs. For the first time in months, I was happy.

The Fatal Night

I danced with Jamie for about an hour that July night. He never stopped grinning from ear to ear. Some people would say this was because of the drug, but I know better.

I'd met Jamie at Hopkins' on-campus pub, where he served beer and watched *Jerry Springer,* and I got to know him better at frat parties, where we'd match up at beer pong, a drinking game. I enjoyed his company at parties and at the bar, but I *loved* being around Jamie at raves. His presence and attitude always made my night. Jamie loved trance music more than anyone I have ever met. As the music built up and crescendoed into anthemic melodies, he would smile and raise a fist into the air. He always found a way to bring the disparate people at raves together—ecstasy users, teetotaling dancers, people just there to hear the music.

After an hour or so I needed to cool off, so I left Jamie on the dance floor and joined friends at the lounge. On the way out of the club, about six hours later, we bumped into Shannon, a girl Jamie had come to Twilo with. She said he'd collapsed on the dance floor and was taken to a hospital. I remember thinking he must have gotten dehydrated; he was probably in the emergency room cooling off and getting juiced up on an IV. It's not uncommon; between the ecstasy, the dancing, and the tropical heat at raves, people get dried out all the time. My friends and I returned to the hotel room we were sharing with another friend, Justin.

At noon the next day, Justin got a call on his cell phone from Shannon. I sat up from my spot on the floor and watched Justin's face fall. He hung up, swallowed once, and repeated what he'd just heard on the phone: Jamie was dead.

Feelings of Guilt

How could someone so big suddenly . . . die? That body always made Jamie seem invincible. Maybe he had thought so too.

None of us cried then. It might have been the shock. Maybe our own ecstasy use the night before had sapped our emotional capabilities for the time being. Whatever the reason, I felt less grief-stricken than confused and empty.

An hour later, Justin was driving me back to the summer camp in southeastern Pennsylvania where I was a bunk counselor, overseeing a group of 15-year-olds. "We have to get you back into a controlled environment," he said—I believe in response to the blank stare on my face.

I spent the next three days acting as if nothing had happened. Then came the funeral. I had been away at camp all summer, rarely seeing my college friends, but they were all there at the funeral. I went thinking I would be strong for them, help them make sense of this tragic loss, but when I saw Jamie's mother at the start of the recession, tears streaming down her cheeks, I dissolved. My friends urged me to talk to Jamie's father, but I felt too guilty. I couldn't shake the feeling that it was our fault—my fault. As the funeral wore on, we all began crying. Here we were, more than 100 of us, crying over the loss of a wonderful person, crying over our own drug use, crying out of fear.

Not all of Jamie's friends were users, of course, and very quickly our circle split into those who did and those who didn't, with the latter asking the former, "Will you ever do it again?" The guilt I'd felt at the funeral kicked back in, redoubled. *Why him?* I asked myself. *Why not me?* I'd used ecstasy dozens of times, Jamie only twice. I was happy when he started, when he joined us. And now he was gone. I became obsessed with the idea that Jamie's death was a sign from God, and I'm not even religious.

No Longer Invincible

I swore off ecstasy, as did some of my previously high-rolling friends. Some talked of starting organizations to inform ravers on the potential hazards of pill-taking, such as the national nonprofit DanceSafe. But I could feel our resolve wavering. I believe that drug use stems from young people's need to feel invincible; a friend once told me that I used ecstasy only because "you like to see yourself on the edge, lying on the floor, f—ked off your ass." To an extent, he was right. I loved losing control. And it didn't take long for us to start rationalizing Jamie's death—to feel safer, to feel invincible, to make ourselves capable of doing it again.

We'd heard Jamie took five pills; a *New York Times* article about his death suggested he also took liquid GHB, another drug popular at raves that has been associated with date rape. This made it easier to deal with—I'd never eaten that many pills or mixed E with another drug. The sad truth is that we'd never know exactly what happened, but I was hearing what I wanted to hear.

Other explanations popped up. I heard Jamie might have had a preexisting heart condition. Overheating was a natural possibility—he was not used to strenuous exercise, and dancing for hours in a packed, saunalike room might have been unsafe for him. Perhaps he didn't rest or drink enough water—

both are factors in heatstroke, the most common cause of ecstasy-related death. I run at least 20 miles a week; overheating and dehydration are less dangerous for me than for someone in Jamie's shape. All these differences and explanations made it easier for us to rationalize our drug use.

With all this churning in my head, I still had to return after the funeral for three more weeks at camp. I talked with only a few people there about what had happened, and then only briefly and superficially. Having used ecstasy weekly for the three months preceding camp, I was already suffering a certain amount of withdrawal before Jamie's death; now the deep sense of shock, loss, and fear was making me hollow. Back in Baltimore, my friends were solving their problems—talking about Jamie, working out their feelings, getting back to normal. By the time I returned from camp, they were talking about rolling again.

Losing the Taste for Ecstasy

On one hand I couldn't believe it—I was really just starting the grieving process. But on the other it was no wonder, no more than it's any wonder that E is the drug of the moment. We live in a world of consumerism and speed, conducting business instantaneously on cell phones and the Internet, globe-trotting on high-speed trains and cheap flights. Why shouldn't we expect to buy bliss? Hello, ecstasy—intellectually empty, but seemingly full of the love and happiness we don't get from buying cars and playing video games. My friends and I weren't naive about the drug, didn't need the likes of *Time* magazine (which sonorously weighed in on the E boom in a June 5 [2000] cover story) to tell us it was dangerous. We knew, and did it anyway. The short-term dangers seemed avoidable— drink water, rest, stay cool, don't overheat. The long-term dangers—depression, memory loss—seemed far, far away.

My first few raves after Jamie's death were sentimental. I went sober, not even drinking. It was hard watching the hundreds of people grinning broadly, rubbing each other, dancing like they were floating on air. After raves when I rolled, I always felt drained but elated; after these, I was just tired and cranky.

The weeks ticked by, but ecstasy strengthened its grip on me even as I eschewed it. The drug might not be physically addictive—for two or three days after a roll the last thing you want to do is take another pill, because your brain doesn't have the serotonin to make it work—but it's extraordinarily addictive psychologically. When you use it regularly, as I did through April, May, and June, life quickly becomes all about the drug.

By early September, I was terribly depressed. But I was also realizing more and more that I never wanted to do ecstasy again. The toxicology reports indicated that Jamie was on ecstasy alone when he died, but it wasn't fear fueling my decision. I'm not scared of doing the drug again—the rationalizing I did after Jamie's death worked all too well—but I do recognize how ecstasy alters emotions and relationships, and I am intimately familiar with its addictive power. I don't want my ups and downs, the way I view people and the way they view me, determined by a little pill. If I'm going to be happy, it's going to have to come from somewhere else.

Jamie's death didn't scare me out of doing ecstasy, but it did make me think about why I had become so enthralled with the magic pill. I don't regret my ecstasy experience; there are things about it I'll remember fondly as well as sadly. But ecstasy is no longer for me. Jamie aside, it cost me too much— my balance, my happiness, and my sense of self.

In Defense of Club Drugs

Jimi Fritz

In this selection, Jimi Fritz, a Canadian musician, writer, and raver, defends the recreational use of club drugs. Many activities are more dangerous than using club drugs such as Ecstasy, he argues, including such seemingly innocuous activities as attending a soccer match in a stadium full of high-spirited fans. He contends that when taken carefully in the correct dosages, club drugs can be safe and enjoyable. Society has been led to believe that any drug not sanctioned by the government for medical purposes is dangerous, Fritz observes. He calls for the legalization of all drugs and an end to the criminalization of recreational drug users.

Drugs are by far the most contentious issue of rave culture and their use at raves is the most touted aspect of the scene and the one most likely to be reported by sensation seeking media. Drugs have always been good copy. Now more than ever, with the US leading the never-ending war on drugs, it seems we must suffer yet another myopic and misguided campaign against one of mankind's most innate and fundamental drives: to expand our consciousness and explore our own psyches.

For thousands of years, human beings have been ingesting various substances to explore the subconscious realms, bring us closer to God, gain insight into the world around us, or to provide relaxation and pleasure. Throughout our long and illustrious history of experimentation there have been relatively few casualties. Until now.

There are many good arguments to support the fact that most of our current problems with drugs, from the crime infested crack houses of Los Angeles to thieving junkies overdosing on bad heroin, are caused by prohibition itself. We have only to study the results of alcohol prohibition in America to know that simply banning a drug does not solve the problems that may be associated with its use, or more accurately, its misuse. Despite [former First Lady] Nancy Reagan's best intentions, just saying no to a symptom does not address the underlying cause. The problems associated with misuse of drugs are always symptomatic of larger social issues.

I believe that most, if not all, of our social ills can be attributed to the breakdown of the family and the isolation of the individual from society as a whole. We have lost our connection to others and therefore, to ourselves. Many people in today's society feel isolated, lost, left out and left behind. Human beings have a fundamental need to feel connected, first to our mothers, then to our families and then to society as a whole. When these connections are fractured or lost all together our lives can quickly become empty and meaningless. We no longer care what happens to others or ourselves. This negative state of mind can soon lead to self-hating and self-destructive behavior.

Drugs are usually not the problem but the symptom. When people lose their way and become desperate they will look for a way out. When no illegal drugs are available, people with problems will drink themselves into oblivion. This is amply demonstrated each and every Saturday night in any city center in the so-called civilized world. If alcohol is not available people will drink after-shave, sniff glue or even guzzle gasoline. These people are displaying aberrant behavior because they have very real psychological problems. When desperate souls can take no more and leap to their death, we do not make tall buildings illegal. If you look into the background of anyone with a drug problem you will invariably find that their dilemma began with a breakdown of some sort in their family or community.

The Public's Fear of Drugs

Mainstream society has been brainwashed into thinking that any drug that is not approved or sanctioned by their government must be harmful. But when we take a look at a "soft" or benign drug such as marijuana and compare it to alcohol or tobacco it is like throwing Minnie Mouse in the ring with [boxer] Mike Tyson. We obviously have some discrepancies in our attitudes and policies towards drugs, and it is about time that we replaced mass hysteria with informed decision-making and begin learning how to use drugs responsibly to enhance and enrich our lives.

Another important thing to keep in mind when dealing with the subject of drugs is what we mean when we use the word "drugs." This word has been bandied about far too freely, and through overuse has become virtually meaningless. It is time we learned to be more specific. No one would argue that penicillin is interchangeable with crack cocaine or that we consider [the poison] strychnine in the same category as coffee. Why then do we use the word "drug" to encompass any substance that may have an effect on our body or mind? The word itself has become synonymous with bad or harmful and is no longer useful as a descriptive term. And while we are on the subject of bad or harmful drugs, let's not forget society's most available and most used drugs: tobacco and alcohol. These two legal drugs alone are responsible for more sickness, deaths, and social ills than all other illegal drugs combined. Recent official Government figures from England report that over one thousand British children under fifteen years of age are hospitalized each year suffering from acute alcohol poisoning and over one hundred and fifty a year die directly from alcohol poisoning. The report also states that twelve per cent of all male deaths in Britain are directly related to alcohol consumption.

One wonders what the reaction would be if the same could be said of ecstasy use. Similar figures around the world have confirmed time and time again that alcohol is without doubt one of the most dangerous and destructive drugs on the planet. But when was the last time you heard anyone calling for a total ban of alcohol? The statistics on tobacco are even worse. The World Health Organization now estimates that up to four million people a year die from tobacco-related diseases!

This is not to say that the psychedelic drugs sometimes used at raves are completely harmless. Any doctor will confirm that drugs are tools and must be used appropriately and responsibly. Thousands upon thousands of people are killed by cars every year but if used properly, an automobile can be a wonderful tool. When misused, it can very quickly be transformed into an instrument of death and destruction. Power tools are completely legal but used improperly can cause some very serious injuries. Our world is full of tools that can be useful or harmful. It is our job as responsible human beings to learn to use tools in a beneficial, rather than a detrimental, way.

Prescription Drugs Can Also Be Dangerous

After decades of dealing—or not dealing—with this issue, it is still difficult to find a public forum in which to exchange ideas on the subject of recreational drug use. You will not find any stories in the newspapers or on television news shows about the positive effects of psychedelic drug use, although the vast majority of users will testify that psychedelics have had extremely positive effects on the quality of their lives. In most societies today it is acceptable to use drugs to relieve pain or mask the symptoms of disease. It is okay to use drugs to wake us up or put us to sleep. We even sanction the use of antipsychotic drugs that improve the mood and temperament of the mentally ill. Prozac, a drug not so distantly related to ecstasy, is now one of the most commonly prescribed drugs in North America.

But there are also significant risks involved with prescription drugs. Many people die every year from adverse reactions to drugs prescribed by their doctor, or problems caused when taking combinations of drugs. For instance, hundreds of people in America die each and every year from allergic reactions to paracetamol. Next time your doctor prescribes a drug for you, ask to see the information from the manufacturer and read the list of possible side effects. Prescription drugs are tested by undergoing a thorough process of double blind studies, and are often approved for public consumption when it has been shown that the benefits outweigh the harmful side effects, which in some cases can be appalling. One look at the recipients of chemotherapy, with its dreadfully low, twenty per cent success rate, will tell you that sometimes the side effects can be far greater than the benefits. In comparison, a drug like ecstasy, which produces a child-like wonder of the world and a feeling of universal love with negligible side effects is still [under Britain's strictest drug law] a class A illegal drug. It is ironic that in a society where the majority of ordinary citizens take drugs for one reason or another, to use a drug to induce pleasure is still considered taboo.

Drugs at the Correct Dosage

Most problems associated with recreational drugs are caused by irresponsible use, i.e., taking them too frequently or in too high a dose. There are no drugs, legal or otherwise, that can be taken in unlimited amounts. All drugs have a correct dosage that, if exceeded, can cause adverse reactions or toxic effects, and the recreational drugs used in the rave scene are no exception. It should be noted that users of psychedelics generally consider them to be special occasion drugs and it would be rare to find anyone taking ecstasy, LSD or magic mushrooms on a daily basis. When used with the right attitude and consumed at the correct dosage and frequency, they can be as safe and enjoyable as a camping trip with the family.

In England alone it is estimated that since 1992, one million doses of ecstasy are consumed each and every week. If we multiply this figure to take into consideration the amount being used by the world population, we have an extremely large sample group. From a group this large there has been only a handful of negative reports. In fact, most of the problems that have been attributed to ecstasy use are usually due to other causes such as overheating caused by insufficient ventilation or overcrowding, dehydration due to the unavailability of water, or problems associated with other, more harmful drugs. One incident in England where a young woman's death was linked to ecstasy was eventually credited to the over-consumption of water, a phenomenon where the blood is diluted and causes tissue cells to swell, creating pressure in the skull. These are all problems that could occur without ecstasy use.

At any large event attended by thousands of people the law of averages will ensure at least a few health problems. People drop dead from heart attacks, heat prostration, strokes and a variety of other reasons at sporting events every year but we do not hear concerned citizens calling for a total ban of football or baseball. The violence at English soccer matches is a good example of our double standards when it comes to how much risk we are willing to tolerate. Every Saturday afternoon in dozens of cities around England there are appalling incidences of soccer violence. Serious injuries and even deaths are common as opposing armies of soccer supporters battle each other in the stadiums and in the streets. The trains used to transport the fans are routinely destroyed and the neighborhoods and towns where the games take place are regularly ransacked. A recent [late 1990s] incidence of soccer violence involving English fans at a game in Belgium resulted in forty-two deaths! This madness presumably continues because the pleasure that the majority of soccer fans get from the game supersedes the injuries and deaths caused by a minority of irresponsible hooligans. If we apply the same logic to raves we would see that the risk factor is negligible in comparison while the enjoyment quota is equal, if not higher. Again, there are no city councils in England calling for a ban of soccer matches.

Ecstasy Is Relatively Safe

Perhaps the English government should rate soccer with their own recently developed system of determining risk factors. If we use the current statistical estimates of consumption from England, the risk of death from ecstasy would be 1 in 6.8 million. In comparison, parachuting kills 3 people in 1000 each year, and skiing kills 1 in 500,000. And if you think that it would be safer to stay at home, think again. The risk of being killed due to an accident in the home is 1 in 26,000 a year. That's over two hundred and fifty times more dangerous than taking a dose of ecstasy. According to the British system, ecstasy use rates the same risk factor as an afternoon of fishing. With dangerous sports like skiing, hang gliding and motor sports, we understand that the inherent risks involved can be extremely high, but at the same time, for some people, the benefits of the excitement and enjoyment outweigh the potential danger. The point is, every activity or drug comes with a risk and we must learn to weigh the risks with the benefits. As anyone who has experienced ecstasy will tell you, the benefits far outweigh the minimal risks.

Recently there has been a growing feeling among the leaders of the world that the war on drugs has been lost and a mountain of statistics from around the globe supports this stance. A United Nations General Assembly Special Session on Drugs was held on June 8–10, 1998, in New York City with an agenda to introduce new strategies to intensify the war on drugs. A petition recommending decriminalization, the introduction of harm reduction policies and other measures to end the war on drugs was sent to the Secretary General of the United Nations, Mr. Kofi Annan. The petition was presented to the assembly on the eve of the meeting and also published in a full-page ad in the *New York Times*. Signed by over six hundred prominent people from forty-one countries, the impressive list included presidents, cabinet ministers, lords, senators, lawyers, ministers, bishops and judges. Even the ex-head of Scotland Yard in England is now publicly calling for the legalization of all drugs, citing the many years of pain and misery he witnessed in the drug squad, which he now sees as a direct effect of prohibition. We can only hope this is a trend which will eventually lead to the end of the persecution and criminalization of recreational drug users, an increase in harm reduction policies and the initiation of programs that address the underlying causes of addiction and other forms of drug abuse.

Rave culture seeks to heal social ills by strengthening our connections to others and therefore ourselves. It is about understanding ourselves so we may better understand others. It is about expanding our hearts and consciousness to see beyond our differences. Rave culture endeavors to promote tolerance and acceptance and the creation of a more positive world. The responsible use of drugs is part of that equation.

CHAPTER THREE

Medical and Legal Issues

The 2001 Ecstasy Prevention Act Will Combat Ecstasy Abuse

Bob Graham

In July 2001 Bob Graham, a Democratic senator from Florida, introduced the Ecstasy Prevention Act in the U.S. Senate. The act (which subsequently passed) was an extension of the Ecstasy Anti-Proliferation Act of 2000, also sponsored by Graham, which strengthened the penalties for trafficking in club drugs. The following selection is taken from Graham's formal introduction of the Ecstasy Prevention Act. His statement outlines the physical and social dangers of the drug and describes the act's provisions for research and law enforcement funding. Graham, who retired from the Senate in 2004 after three terms, attempted to become a Democratic presidential nominee in the 2004 election but later withdrew from the race.

Mr. President, I rise today, along with my colleagues, Senators [Charles] Grassley, [Joseph] Lieberman, [Dick] Durbin, [Mary] Landrieu, and [Hillary] Clinton, to introduce the Ecstasy Prevention Act of 2001: legislation to combat the recent rise in trafficking, distribution and violence associated with MDMA, a club drug commonly known as Ecstasy. Ecstasy has become the "feel good" drug of choice among many of our young people, and drug pushers are marketing it as a "friendly" drug

Bob Graham, statement before the U.S. Senate Committee on the Judiciary, Washington, DC, July 19, 2001.

to mostly teenagers and young adults.

Last year [2000] I sponsored and Congress passed legislation [the Ecstasy Anti-Proliferation Act] which drew attention
to the dangers of Ecstasy and strengthened the penalties attached to trafficking in Ecstasy and other "club drugs." Since
then, Ecstasy use and trafficking continue to grow at epidemic
proportions, and there are many accounts of deaths and permanent damage to the health of those who use Ecstasy. The
U.S. Customs Service continues to report large increases in Ecstasy seizures; over 9 million pills were seized by Customs last
year, a dramatic rise from the 400,000 seized in 1997. According to the United States Customs Service, in Fiscal Year 2001,
two individual seizures affected by Customs Inspectors in Miami, FL totaled approximately 422,000 Ecstasy tablets. These
two seizures alone exceeded the entire amount of ecstasy
seized by the Customs Service in all of Fiscal Year 1997. The
Deputy Director of the Office of National Drug Control Policy
[ONDCP], Dr. Donald Vereen, Jr., M.D., M.P.H., recently said
that "Ecstasy is one of the most problematic drugs that has
emerged in recent years." The National Drug Intelligence Center, in its most recent publication *Threat Assessment 2001*, has
noted that "no drug in the Other Dangerous Drugs Category
represents a more immediate threat than MDMA" or Ecstasy.

The Office of National Drug Control Policy's *Year 2000 Annual Report on the National Drug Control Strategy* clearly states
that the use of Ecstasy is on the rise in the United States, particularly among teenagers and young professionals. My State of
Florida has been particularly hard hit by this plague, but so
have the States of many of my colleagues here. Ecstasy is cus-
tomarily sold and consumed at "raves," which are semi-
clandestine, all-night parties and concerts. Numerous data also
reflect the increasing availability of Ecstasy in metropolitan
centers and suburban communities. In the most recent release
of *Pulse Check: Trends in Drug Abuse Mid–Year 2000*, which featured MDMA and club drugs, it was reported that the sale and
use of club drugs have expanded from raves and nightclubs to

high schools, streets, neighborhoods and other open venues.

Not only has the use of Ecstasy exploded, more than doubling among 12th graders in the last two years, but it has also spread well beyond its origin as a party drug for affluent white suburban teenagers to virtually every ethnic and class group, and from big cities like New York and Los Angeles to rural Vermont and South Dakota.

Ecstasy Spreads to Violent Venues

And now, this year [2001], law enforcement officials say they are seeing another worrisome development, increasingly violent turf wars among Ecstasy dealers, and some of those dealers are our young people. Homicides linked to Ecstasy dealing have occurred in recent months in Norfolk, VA; Elgin, IL, near Chicago; and in Valley Stream, NY. Police suspect Ecstasy in

These Ecstasy tablets were seized by U.S. Customs officials. The 2001 Ecstasy Prevention Act was designed to stop the flow of club drugs into the United States.

other murders in the suburbs of Washington, DC, and Los Angeles, and violence is being linked to Israeli drug dealers in Los Angeles and to organized crime in New York City. Ecstasy is also becoming widely available on the Internet. Last year, a man arrested in Orlando, FL, had been selling Ecstasy to customers in New York.

The lucrative nature of Ecstasy encourages its importation. Production costs are as low as two to twenty-five cents per dose while retail prices in the U.S. range from twenty dollars to $45 per dose. Manufactured mostly in Europe, in nations such as the Netherlands, Belgium, and Spain where pill presses are not controlled as they are in the U.S., Ecstasy has erased all of the old routes law enforcement has mapped out for the smuggling of traditional drugs. And now the trade is being promoted by organized criminal elements, both from abroad and here. Although Israeli and Russian groups dominate MDMA smuggling, the involvement of domestic groups appears to be increasing. Criminal groups based in Chicago, Phoenix, Texas, and Florida have reportedly secured their own sources of supply in Europe.

Ecstasy Is Not Harmless

Young Americans are being lulled into a belief that Ecstasy, and other designer drugs, are "safe" ways to get high, escape reality, and enhance intimacy in personal relationships. The drug traffickers make their living off of perpetuating and exploiting this myth.

I want to be perfectly clear in stating that Ecstasy is an extremely dangerous drug. In my State alone, between July and December of last year [2000], there were 25 deaths in which MDMA or a variant were listed as a cause of death, and there were another 25 deaths where MDMA was present in the toxicology, although not actually listed as the cause of death. This drug is a definite killer.

The Ecstasy Prevention Act of 2001 renews and enhances

our commitment toward fighting the proliferation and trafficking of Ecstasy and other club drugs. It builds on last year's Ecstasy Anti-Proliferation Act of 2000 and provides legislation to assist the Federal and local organizations that are fighting to stop this potentially life-threatening drug. This legislation will allot funding for programs that will educate law enforcement officials and young people and will assist community-based anti-drug efforts. To that end, this bill amends Section 506B(c) of Title V of the Public Health Service Act, by adding that priority of funding should be given to communities that have taken measures to combat club drug trafficking and use, to include passing ordinances and increasing law enforcement on Ecstasy.

The bill also provides money for the National Institute on Drug Abuse to conduct research and evaluate the effects that MDMA or Ecstasy has on an individual's health. And, because there is a fear that the lack of current drug tests' ability to screen for Ecstasy may encourage Ecstasy use over other drugs, the bill directs ONDCP to commission a test for Ecstasy that meets the standards of and can be used in the Federal Workplace.

Hope to Reduce Ecstasy Use

Through this campaign, our hope is that Ecstasy will soon go the way of crack, which saw a dramatic reduction in the quantities present on our streets after information of its unpredictable impurities and side effects were made known to a wide audience. By using this educational effort we hope to avoid future deaths and ruined lives.

The Ecstasy Prevention Act of 2001 can only help in our fight against drug abuse in the United States. Customs is working hard to stem the flow of Ecstasy into our country. As legislators we have a responsibility to stop the proliferation of this potentially life-threatening drug. The Ecstasy Prevention Act of 2001 will assist the Federal and local agencies charged to fight drug abuse by raising the public profile on the substance-abuse challenge posed by the increasing availability and use of Ecstasy and by focusing on the serious danger it presents to our youth.

We urge our colleagues in the Senate to join us in this important effort by co-sponsoring this bill.

The 2001 Ecstasy Prevention Act Violates Civil Liberties

Greg Smith

The Ecstasy Prevention Act, which Congress passed in 2001, provides increased federal public health funding for communities working to reduce Ecstasy use. In this selection Greg Smith argues that the act unfairly targets the rave subculture because communities that pass laws to restrict rave clubs receive priority funding. It is unconstitutional for law enforcement agencies to single out one group of people based on the kind of music they listen to, Smith writes. He also notes that the public health funds spent on what he considers a futile war against drug use could be better spent on helping people to overcome their drug addictions. Smith was the opinion editor of the *On-Line 49er* newspaper when he wrote this article.

Our civil liberties are being violated at the expense of the government-declared "War on Drugs." It is a fundamental right and an individual choice to control one's own consciousness.

The popularity of MDMA, or Ecstasy, has skyrocketed and while the education of Ecstasy's negative health effects, as well as its benefits, needs to be emphasized, officials have placed ignorant stereotypes on a specific subculture: music. In the last year [since 2001], ordinances restricting parties, shutting down clubs and seizing lands designated as "high inten-

---

Greg Smith, "Ecstasy Act Step in Wrong Direction," *On-Line 49er*, www.csulb.edu/~d49er, vol. 9, February 6, 2002. Copyright © 2002 by Daily Forty-Niner. All rights reserved. Reproduced by permission.

sity drug trafficking areas" under Crackhouse laws and the Ecstasy Prevention Act of 2001 have been crunching down on the electronic music scene.

The Ecstasy Prevention Act, introduced by Sen. Bob Graham, D-Fla., was passed last December [2001] to aid in the specific war on Ecstasy and other "club drugs." By targeting one subculture, not only is one music scene being unconstitutionally scrutinized, cultural stereotypes are being perpetuated. Because law enforcement agencies cannot identify Ecstasy users based on violent behavior, they are left to rely on the style of music people listen to.

Drug Laws and Prejudice

Under Section 8002 of the act, communities that pass ordinances "restricting rave clubs" and increase law enforcement efforts directed toward Ecstasy offenders will receive priority in funding under the Public Health Service Act. Public health funds should not be based on a community giving in to pressures to squash a particular subculture.

Last month [January 2002], the California Senate killed two identical bills with a 3-2 vote in opposition that threatened to impose a 90-day mandatory minimum sentence for using or being under the influence of Ecstasy. There is still opportunity for these bills to move forward.[1] This is not the answer we are looking for. Sections 8003 and 8007 of the Ecstasy Prevention Act authorize the use of $16 million to assist in law enforcement initiatives and to establish a federal task force against MDMA and other club drugs. Instead of wasting this money on a futile War on Drugs policy, we should be educating children for hopeful prevention, not ripping them out of schools and locking them up.

Last Sunday [February 3, 2002], Super Bowl audiences were exposed to the propaganda of the Office of National Drug Con-

1. The bills died in the Senate in 2002.

trol Policy: "If you use illegal drugs, then you support terrorism." Does this mean non-drug users support patriotism? Terrorism is defined in *Webster's New World Dictionary* as "the use of force or threats to intimidate, etc., especially as a political policy." What, then, does one support when terrorism is used to spread propaganda of patriotic values?

The [drug legalization advocate] Alchemind Society noted the most disturbing facet of the multi-million-dollar campaign: the magnitude of advertising costs. The average cost for a full year of methadone maintenance treatment is $4,700 a patient. The costs of these two ad spots at $1.6 million each, not including production costs, could have treated 680 heroin addicts, the Alchemind Society reported.

Illegal Drugs Are Not the Only Dangerous Drugs

But no one's saying much about the 10 ad spaces [brewery] Anheuser-Busch Co. wedged in. Oh, but that's right, alcohol isn't a drug. It doesn't alter consciousness or kill thousands each year. Alcohol is only involved in almost four out of 10 violent crimes as well as four out of 10 motor vehicle accidents, according to a 1998 U.S. Department of Justice report. It makes profits for American companies, so we'll just leave it alone with nicotine and caffeine.

Worldwide, 180 million people use illegal drugs, according to the United Nations. The National Drug Intelligence Center reports that 3.3 million Americans admitted in 1998 that they have used MDMA, and last year [2001] U.S. Customs seized 9.3 million MDMA pills. These statistics suggest the widespread desire to experience alternative states of consciousness.

The decision to alter one's consciousness should be left to the individual's discretion, without consequential effects on any collective whole that gathers peacefully.

The RAVE Act Is Unconstitutional

Brooke A. Levy

First introduced in June 2002, the Reducing Americans' Vulnerability to Ecstasy (RAVE) Act initially failed to pass the Senate. However, in April 2003 supporters of the act attached a slightly altered version of it, renamed the Illicit Drug Anti-Proliferation Act, to the unrelated AMBER Alert Bill intended to improve response to child abductions. The Senate was eager to pass the AMBER Alert Bill, and as a result, the new RAVE Act became law. According to the legislation, individuals who knowingly allow drug use, distribution, or manufacture on their property will be held criminally and civilly liable. The penalties include a prison sentence of up to twenty years and fines of up to $250,000. The sponsors of the act state that it is intended to curtail raves and the use of club drugs. In this selection, Brooke A. Levy argues that the act violates free speech, punishes the innocent, and might drive raves to dangerous, underground settings. Since the act punishes property owners for the use of illegal drugs on their premises, she asserts, the owners will be forced to completely ban raves and other events on their property in order to protect themselves from liability. The act is thus an infringement on citizens' constitutional right to freedom of speech, Levy concludes. Levy is associate editor for the *Northwestern University Law Review*.

Until recently, the RAVE Act [Reducing Americans' Vulnerability to Ecstasy] represented the government's most aggressive

Brooke A. Levy, "When Cute Acronyms Happen to Bad Legislation: The Reducing Americans' Vulnerability to Ecstasy 'RAVE' Act," *Northwestern University Law Review*, vol. 98, Spring 2004, p. 1,251. Copyright © 2004 by the Northwestern University School of Law. Reproduced by permission.

action yet to curb the use of club drugs and attack the party scene in general. On a federal level, the opposition to rave-style parties and their promoters had been building, but the last congressional measure, which passed in December 2001, proved less drastic. Entitled the Ecstasy Prevention Act, the Act gave "states financial incentives for passing ordinances restricting rave clubs and seizing land used for raves via nuisance laws."

On June 18, 2002, Senator Joseph Biden, a Democrat from Delaware, introduced the RAVE Act to the Senate. A paramount crusader in the War on Drugs, Senator Biden serves as chair of both the International Narcotics Control Caucus and the Judiciary Subcommittee on Crime and Drugs. His proposal, the RAVE Act, declared that "it shall be unlawful to"

(1) knowingly open, *lease, rent*, use or maintain any place, whether permanently *or temporarily;* and

(2) manage or control any place, whether permanently *or temporarily*, either as an owner, lessee, agent, employee, occupant, or mortgagee, and knowingly and intentionally rent, lease, profit from, or make available for use, with or without compensation, the place for the purpose of unlawfully manufacturing, storing, distributing, or using a controlled substance. [emphasis added]

The Act, an extension of the 1986 Crack House Statute, subjects violators to a civil penalty of either $250,000 or "2 times the gross receipts, either known or estimated, that were derived from each violation that is attributable to the person," as well as declaratory and injunctive remedies. Furthermore, the civil penalty is in addition to already existing criminal penalties of up to twenty years' imprisonment and a possible $500,000 fine.

The Initial Backlash

Immediately following the bill's introduction on June 18, 2002, there was a large and relatively successful outcry from the ACLU [American Civil Liberties Union], the electronic music community, and the public at large. Claiming that the bill violated basic constitutional rights, the ACLU argued that citizens should "urge [their] senators to oppose attacks on youth culture." One ACLU official [Lou Chibbaro] called the legislation "a draconian measure that would have a 'chilling effect' on club owners and promoters, prompting them to discontinue holding raves and circuit parties." Another official alleged that "holding club owners and promoters of raves criminally liable for what some people may do at these events is no different from arresting the stadium owners and promoters of a Rolling Stones concert or a rap show because some concert-goers may be smoking or selling marijuana."

The efforts of many activist groups successfully blocked the RAVE Act from becoming law in 2002. In 2003, however, the supporters of the drug war bill came back with a vengeance. They stopped calling the bill the "RAVE Act," sticking the Act's exact same provisions into a miscellaneous domestic security bill sponsored by Senator Tom Daschle. The new provisions, like the RAVE Act, revised the federal "crack house law" to improve the ease with which federal prosecutors could fine and imprison innocent business owners who failed to stop drug offenses from occurring on their property.

The new home of the RAVE Act, Senate Bill S. 22, was introduced on January 9, 2003, as the Justice Enhancement and Domestic Security Act of 2003. As explained in the introductory remarks by the senators who proposed the legislation, the bill was a catch-all or "comprehensive" crime bill that built "on prior Democratic crime initiatives . . . that worked [in the past] to bring the crime rate down." The bill contained seven broad-ranging sections, including Title V, which pertained to "Combating Drug and Gun Violence." Within this Title was Part 4, labeled the "Crack House Statute Amendments." This Part, while no longer distinctly labeled the RAVE Act, laid out the exact same changes to the Crack House Statute as the RAVE Act did. In short, the new provisions (even under a disguised heading) still threatened First Amendment rights and innocent business owners.

The RAVE Act Passes

Adding the RAVE Act to the Justice Enhancement and Domestic Security Act of 2003 did not help the legislation become law. In fact, supporters of the RAVE Act had to hide its provisions one more time, in an even more questionable place, in order for Congress to pass the Act. In April 2003, Senator Biden, at the very last minute, added the provisions of the RAVE Act to the unrelated AMBER Alert bill, which was proposed in the wake of . . . [the] Elizabeth Smart [child abduction case] and as a result of the country's desire to quickly respond to the growing problem of child abduction. The AMBER Alert bill, a bill to prevent child abduction and the sexual exploitation of children, became part of a piece of legislation entitled the PROTECT Act (again, a very cute acronym, "Prosecutorial Remedies and Other Tools to end the Exploitation of Children Today Act"). Under Title VI of the PROTECT Act, "Miscellaneous Provisions," Senator Biden added the RAVE Act provisions, retitled this time as the "Illicit Drug Anti-Proliferation Act." On April 30, President [George W.] Bush signed the PROTECT Act into law, thus making the RAVE Act Public Law 108-21.

While ravers describe raves as "life changing" and "religious" experiences, supporters of the RAVE Act appear to view raves solely as part of a dangerous culture that promotes drug use. Because raves tend to be associated with drugs, especially ecstasy, supporters of the RAVE Act believe that the Act can curb ecstasy use by punishing all individuals who make raves possible. According to ravers and civil rights activists, however, by increasing sentencing guidelines and the number of people who can be held responsible for a rave, the Act is not just designed to curb the prevalence of ecstasy use, but also to completely wipe out the existence of raves and rave culture.

Since April 2003, when the RAVE Act passed as part of the AMBER Alert bill ("PROTECT Act"), two additional pieces of legislation have surfaced. The Ecstasy Awareness Act and the CLEAN-UP Act threaten to widen the laws to prosecute anyone who holds an event and fails, even with a valid attempt, to prevent illicit drug use. [As of early 2005, Congress had not taken action on either act. However, promoters of the CLEAN-UP Act had removed a section making live-music venues liable for customers' drug use.] Similar to the RAVE Act, the two new pieces of legislation raise constitutional issues. They demonstrate that the Supreme Court, if presented with the issue, should declare the RAVE Act unconstitutional in order to put an end to these draconian measures. . . .

The RAVE Act and Free Speech

Following the [2002 *McClure v. Ashcroft*] holding [that the banning of rave-associated items at public events violated free speech], Graham Boyd, Director of the ACLU's Drug Policy Litigation Project, declared that this "decision should send a message to government that the way to combat illegal substance abuse is not through intimidation and nonsensical laws." Boyd said that the decision "tells law enforcement agents that if you want to target drug use at raves, you've got to play by the rules. Go after the drug dealers, not the entertainers and dancers and people who are there to enjoy the show." Joe Cook, the Executive Director of the ACLU of Louisiana, also embraced the Court's unequivocal protection of First Amendment freedom of speech rights. Cook stated, "[w]e the people should rejoice in this blow for our rights and not allow any of our freedoms to become a casualty in the war on drugs.". . .

The analysis as to whether the RAVE Act violates the First Amendment's guarantee of free speech looks almost identical to the court's analysis in *McClure v. Ashcroft*. While *McClure* addressed banning items associated with enhancing the effects of drugs at raves in order to curb ecstasy use, the RAVE Act takes *McClure* one step further. Rather than merely banning items used at raves in order to reduce ecstasy use, the RAVE Act actually attempts to ban raves altogether in order to reduce ecstasy use. By broadly threatening providers of electronic music, among others, the RAVE Act practically shuts down electronic concerts known as raves and eliminates a form of expression simply because the form of expression is associated with drug use.

As in *McClure v. Ashcroft*, the first question a court would likely address is whether the speech targeted by the RAVE Act is actually protected by the First Amendment. Because the RAVE Act virtually abolishes raves, the two main components of raves, electronic music and dance, would have to be protected under the First Amendment. . . .

In *McClure*, the court . . . found that dancing at raves is protected by the First Amendment. With regard to the electronic music component, the Supreme Court, in *Ward v. Rock Against Racism* [1984], addressed music as generally receiving free speech protection under the First Amendment. The Supreme Court held:

> Music is one of the oldest forms of human expression. From Plato's discourse in the *Republic* to the totalitarian state in our own times, rulers have known its capacity to appeal to the intellect and to the emotions, and have censored musical compositions to serve the needs of the state. The Constitution prohibits any like attempts in our own legal order. Music, as any form of expression and communication, is protected under the First Amendment.

Based on *Ward*, electronic music thus should be protected by the First Amendment. Similar to dance at raves, electronic music can convey myriad messages such as freedom, peace, and identification with a culture. . . .

The Problem of Vague Wording

In addition to the argument that the Supreme Court should find the RAVE Act unconstitutional on free speech grounds, the Supreme Court should also find the RAVE Act unconstitutional by means of the void for vagueness doctrine. Excessively vague laws violate due process regardless of whether speech is regulated; however, courts are especially troubled by vague laws that restrict speech because they threaten to chill constitutionally protected speech. "The Court has observed that freedom of speech is 'delicate and vulnerable, as well as supremely precious in our society . . . [and that] the threat of sanctions may deter their exercise almost as potently as the actual application of sanctions.'"

In *Grayned v. City of Rockford* [1972], the Supreme Court stated that "[i]t is a basic principle of due process that an enactment is void for vagueness if its prohibitions are not clearly defined." The Court then explained the three most important values that vague laws offend. First, the Court affirmed that "because we assume that man is free to steer between lawful and unlawful conduct, *we insist that laws give the person of ordinary intelligence a reasonable opportunity to know what is prohibited, so that he may act accordingly.* [emphasis added] Vague laws may trap the innocent by not providing fair warning." Second, the Court stated that laws must provide explicit standards for those who apply them in order to prevent arbitrary and discriminatory enforcement. "A vague law impermissibly delegates basic policy matters to policemen, judges, and juries for resolution on an ad hoc and subjective basis, with the attendant dangers of arbitrary and discriminatory application." Finally, the Court explained, "where a vague statute abuts upon sensitive areas of basic First Amendment Freedoms, it operates to inhibit the exercise of those freedoms. Uncertain meanings inevitably lead citizens to steer far wider of the unlawful zone than if the boundaries of the forbidden areas were clearly marked.". . .

Although the RAVE Act specifically tries to target ecstasy and raves, it actually creates a non-objective law because the language is so vague that it renders it impossible for anyone to know what specific conduct will make him or her liable under the law. Unlike the current crack house statute, which requires "permanency," the RAVE Act declares that an owner is liable if his premises are only "temporarily" used for drug purposes. According to author S.M. Oliva, "[t]his one word actually negates the entire purpose of the crack-house law in the first place! A crack-house is supposed to be a building or property whose purpose is to facilitate drug use. The purpose of a concert is to, well, entertain people with musical performances. That's not illegal." However, under the RAVE Act, even if only one person is using drugs at a show, the use technically can create civil and criminal liability for the owner.

Further Opposition to the RAVE Act

In effect, the RAVE Act allows federal prosecutors to target other events, such as hip hop or country music concerts, and other places drug offenses occur. As Graham Boyd, Director of the American Civil Liberties Union Drug Policy Litigation Project, testified before the House Judiciary Subcommittee on Crime, Terrorism, and Homeland Security, the RAVE Act could

> apply to hotel and motel owners, cruise ship operators, stadium owners, landlords, real estate managers, and even promoters. It is so broadly written that anyone who used drugs in their own home or threw an event (such as a party or barbeque) in which one or more of their guests used drugs could potentially face a $500,000 fine and up to twenty years in federal prison. If the offense occurred in a hotel room or on a cruise ship, the owner of the property could also go to jail.

Thus, based on its vagueness, the RAVE Act will likely create exactly what the Supreme Court's void for vagueness doctrine in *Grayned* attempted to eliminate—legislation that delegates too much power "to policemen, judges, and juries for resolution on an ad hoc and subjective basis, with the attendant dangers of arbitrary and discriminatory application."

In September 2002, some of the Senators who originally supported the RAVE Act became aware of the Act's vagueness. On September 13, 2002, Senator Patrick Leahy withdrew his support of the RAVE Act based entirely on this problem. Leahy stated, "[a] more narrowly crafted bill to target only unscrupulous promoters who are purposely holding events in order to profit from the illegal distribution of ecstasy and other illegal drugs to young people would be preferable." For much the same reason, Senator Richard Durbin followed Leahy's lead and, on September 24, 2002, withdrew his support of the bill. Following the Act's passage in April 2003, the likelihood of the RAVE Act violating First Amendment rights due to its vagueness became even more apparent and possibly even substantiated. On June 10, 2003, not even one month after President Bush signed the Act into law, the Drug Reform Coordination Network reported that a fundraising concert for the Montana chapter of the National Organization for the Reform of Marijuana Laws ("NORML") was cancelled, just hours before the event was to begin. According to press, a DEA [Drug Enforcement Administration] agent presented the venue's managers with a copy of the RAVE Act and "threatened them with hefty fines and property forfeiture if any drugs were found on the premises during the fundraiser." According to Allen St. Pierre, NORML's executive director, "the intimidation created the desired effect: scaring the club owners into canceling the fundraiser." St. Pierre stated that the DEA agent "absolutely, positively spelled it out to the management of the club that they could be in violation of this brand-spanking-new law." St. Pierre also charged that "the agents, knowing the fundraiser was intended to support drug policy reform groups, stifled the groups' free speech rights by pre-emptively [sic] shutting down the event."

The above situation illustrates the fear that opponents to the RAVE Act have voiced since its proposal—that the RAVE Act allows the government to immediately and proactively prohibit gatherings of people with views with which the government disagrees: as one article [in BBS News] summarized in its title, "Biden's Sneaky Rave Act Draws First Blood." Although Senator Biden and other RAVE Act supporters assured opponents that the Act would not be applied in this manner, actions speak louder than words. It is now even clearer that the public must worry about the Act's vagueness. . . .

If raves ended as they currently exist, the rave scene would likely just move underground into basements, parks, and abandoned buildings. As one director of public relations and marketing for a rave production company stated, "It's sad when every year we hear about a dozen or so deaths due to ecstasy. . . . But the thought of two thousand people at a party at an underground warehouse with no air conditioning, no fire escapes, no sprinkler systems—that terrifies me. [The RAVE Act] creates way more problems than it solves." In fact, many of the casualties reported at raves occur due to overheating caused by overcrowding and poor ventilation.

The Supreme Court should prohibit the RAVE Act because the ramifications of the Act may quite possibly outweigh the benefits. Because ravers will likely fight for rave culture to exist—and have done so even since the passage of the Act—the Act probably will just make raves less safe. Either rave promoters will stop providing necessary safety measures, or raves will move further underground into locations that are more dangerous. In accordance with public policy, the Supreme Court should not support legislation that causes further danger to the young people it purports to protect.

Defending the RAVE Act

Joseph R. Biden Jr.

As chairman of the Judiciary Subcommittee on Crime and Drugs, Democratic senator Joseph R. Biden Jr. introduced the Reducing Americans' Vulnerability to Ecstasy (RAVE) Act in 2002. The act, which held property owners responsible for the use of controlled substances, including club drugs, on their property, initially failed to pass in Congress. However, the act was renamed the Illicit Drug Anti-Proliferation Act and was passed in 2003 as part of the Prosecutorial Remedies and Other Tools to End the Exploitation of Children Today (PROTECT) Act, more commonly known as the AMBER Alert Act, which is designed to help rescue children who have been abducted.

This selection, taken from a speech made by Biden before the Senate in July 2003, defends the RAVE Act against critics who claim that the law will result in unfair prosecution of property owners. Biden argues that under the law, only owners who *knowingly* allow their property to be used for drug sale, use, or manufacture will be prosecuted. He also states that the purpose of his bill is to help to prosecute people who hold events such as raves with the intention of promoting illegal drug use.

Biden has served on the U.S. Senate since 1972.

The Illicit Drug Anti-Proliferation Act [the RAVE Act], legislation which I authored, became law as part of the PROTECT [Prosecutorial Remedies and Other Tools to End the Exploitation of

---

Joseph R. Biden Jr., statement before the U.S. Senate, Washington, DC, July 31, 2003.

Children Today] Act in April [2003]. The bill provides Federal prosecutors the tools needed to combat the manufacture, distribution or use of any controlled substance at any venue whose purpose is to engage in illegal narcotics activity. Rather than create a new law, it merely amends a well-established statute to make clear that anyone who knowingly and intentionally uses their property—or allows another person to use their property—for the purpose of distributing or manufacturing or using illegal drugs can be held accountable, regardless of whether the drug use is ongoing or occurs at a single event.

I introduced this legislation after holding a series of hearings regarding the dangers of Ecstasy and the rampant drug promotion associated with some raves. For the past few years Federal prosecutors have been using the so-called "crack house statute"—a law which makes it illegal for someone to knowingly and intentionally hold an event for the purpose of drug use, distribution or manufacturing—to prosecute rogue rave promoters who profit off of putting kids at risk. My bill simply amended that existing law in two ways. First, it made the "crack house statute" apply not just to ongoing drug distribution operations, but to "single-event" activities, including an event where the promoter has as his primary purpose the sale of Ecstasy or other illegal drugs. And second, it made the law apply to outdoor as well as indoor activity.

Although this legislation grew out of the problems identified at raves, the criminal and civil penalties in the bill would also apply to people who promoted any type of event for the purpose of illegal drug manufacturing, sale, or use. This said, it is important to recognize that this legislation is not designed in any way, shape or form to hamper the activities of legitimate event promoters. If rave promoters and sponsors operate such events as they are so often advertised—as places for people to come dance in a safe, drug-free environment—then they have nothing to fear from this law. In no way is this bill aimed at stifling any type of music or expression—it is only trying to deter illicit drug use and protect kids.

The Act Is Not Designed to Prosecute Law-Abiding Owners

I know that there will always be certain people who will bring drugs into musical or other events and use them without the knowledge or permission of the promoter or club owner. This is not the type of activity that my bill addresses. The purpose of my legislation is not to prosecute legitimate law-abiding managers of stadiums, arenas, performing arts centers, licensed beverage facilities and other venues because of incidental drug use at their events. In fact, when crafting this legislation, I took steps to ensure that it did not capture such cases. My bill would help in the prosecution of rogue promoters who intentionally hold the event for the purpose of illegal drug use or distribution. That is quite a high bar.

I am committed to making sure that this law is enforced properly and have been in close contact with officials from the Drug Enforcement Administration [DEA] to make sure that the law is property construed. That is why I was concerned by press reports about a DEA Agent in Billings, Montana who misinterpreted the Illicit Drug Anti-Proliferation Act when he approached the manager of the local Eagles Lodge to warn her that she may be violating the new law if the Lodge allowed the National Organization to Reform Marijuana Laws (NORML) to have a fundraiser at their facility.

I was troubled to hear this because, according to press reports, the Eagles Lodge had no knowledge that there might be drug activity at their location before the DEA approached them. And following the DEA Agent's misguided advice based on an inaccurate understanding of the law, the Lodge decided to cancel the NORML event, leading to an outcry from various groups that the new law has stifled free speech.

As I mentioned, the law only applies to those who "knowingly and intentionally" hold an event "for the purpose of" drug manufacturing, sale and use. Based upon my understanding of the facts around the NORML fundraising incident, the Eagles Lodge did not come anywhere close to violating that high legal standard.

Correcting a Misinterpretation

I had my staff meet with the DEA chief counsel's office to discuss the Eagles Lodge incident and DEA's interpretation of the law. The DEA assured by office that they shared my understanding of the law and that this interpretation of the statue was conveyed to all DEA field offices shortly after the bill was signed into law.

In a June 19, 2003, letter to me from DEA Acting Administrator William B. Simpkins, the DEA acknowledged that the Special Agent "misinterpreted" DEA's initial legal guidance on the law and "incorrectly" suggested to the Eagles Lodge that the law might apply to the NORML fundraiser. DEA conceded that "[r]egrettably, the DEA Special Agent's incorrect interpretation of the statute contributed to the decision of the Eagles Lodge to cancel the event." In response to this misguided interpretation of the law, the DEA issued on June 17, 2003, supplemental guidance in a memo to all DEA field agents making clear that property owners not personally involved in illicit drug activity would not be violating the Act unless they knowingly and intentionally permitted on their property an event primarily for the purpose of drug use. Legitimate property owners and event promoters would not be violating the Act simply based upon or just because of illegal patron behavior.

I have expressed clearly to Ms. [Karen] Tandy [DEA administrator] my expectation that the law will be applied narrowly and responsibly. Ms. Tandy has confirmed that under her direction the DEA will implement the law as it was intended, targeting only those events whose promoters knowingly and intentionally allow the manufacture, sale or use of illegal drugs. In the DEA's June 19, 2003, letter to me, it noted that its initial May 15, 2003, guidance informed [DEA] personnel that [the law's] requirements of "knowledge" and "intent" were not changed by the [new] Act. Accordingly, legitimate event promoters, such as bona fide managers of stadiums, arenas, performing arts centers, and licensed beverage facilities, should not be concerned that they will be prosecuted simply based upon or just because of illegal patron activity.

Obviously, DEA's May 15th guidance was not sufficient to prevent the unfortunate Eagles Lodge incident but it reveals the Agency's understanding and intent not to target and prosecute the sorts of legitimate businesses cited above. As this is a new law, Ms. Tandy agrees that DEA must and will redouble its efforts in training its agents on the proper legal interpretation.

Answering the Critics

Finally, let me conclude by making two final responses to some critics of my law who have claimed, one, that it stretches the law beyond its original intention, and two, that it creates a legal standard that will permit innocent businessmen, concert promoters, even homeowners to be prosecuted for the drug use of those who come to their property. Both charges are wrong, as I will now explain.

First, my law amended section 856 of Title 21, U.S. Code. Section 856 became law in 1986. While section 856 has become known popularly as the "crack house statute," it has always been available to prosecute any venue—not just crack houses—where the owner knowingly and intentionally made the property available for the purpose of illegal activity. This fact has long been recognized by the Federal courts. As the Ninth Circuit Court of Appeals—the most liberal Federal appellate court in the nation—said: "There is no reason to believe that [section 856] was intended to apply only to storage facilities and crack houses.". . . Or, in the words of the Fifth Circuit Court of Appeals: "it is highly unlikely that anyone would openly maintain a place for the purpose of manufacturing and distributing cocaine without some sort of 'legitimate' cover—as a residence, a nightclub, a retail business, or a storage barn.". . .

The suggestion by some that my law expanded section 856 to entities other than traditional crack houses is simply untrue. Rather, in the 17 years section 856 has been on the books, it has been used by the Justice Department to prosecute seemingly "legitimate businesses" used as a front for drug activity. Specifically, section 856 has been used against motels, bars, restaurants, used car dealerships, apartments, private clubs, and taverns. . . .

The bottom line is that if a defendant hides behind the front of a legitimate business, or allows a drug dealer to do so on their property, they should be held accountable. Just as the criminal law punishes the defendant who "aids and abets"— like the getaway driver in a bank robbery ring—section 856 has always punished those who knowingly and intentionally provide a venue for others to engage in illicit drug activity.

The New Law Does Not Make It Easier to Prosecute People

The second point I will make is that my law does not—does not—change the well-established legal standard of section 856 which is required to secure a criminal conviction. Some critics of my law suggest that Congress just created a new, incredibly low legal threshold for prosecution under my law. In fact, it is the exact opposite. For 17 years [since 1986], section 856 has required a high burden of proof, and my law does not change that standard at all. So let's get our facts straight.

In order to convict a defendant under section 856, the Justice Department needs to prove 2 things beyond a reasonable doubt—the highest legal standard in our justice system. Specifically, the government must prove that the defendant, one, "knowingly and intentionally" made their property available, and two, "for the purpose" of illegal drug distribution, manufacture or use. These are 2 high hurdles the government must first pass before a defendant can be convicted under section 856. Let me briefly discuss both of these legal elements. As will become quite clear, the Federal courts interpreting section 856 have consistently rejected the very broad interpretations of the statute many critics now assert will result from my law.

Federal courts construing the "knowledge" and "intent" prong of section 856 have consistently held this to be a very high bar. It's not enough for a defendant to simply think, or have reason to believe, that drug use could occur on their property. Actual knowledge of future drug use, coupled with a specific intention that such use occur, is required. One Federal court discussing the knowing and intentional standard put it this way: an act is done "knowingly" if done voluntarily and intentionally, and not because of mistake or accident or other innocent reason. The purpose of adding the word "knowingly" is to insure that no one will be convicted for an act done because of mistake or accident, or other innocent reason. Actual knowledge on the part of the defendant that she was renting, leasing or making available for use the [property] for the purpose of unlawfully storing, distributing, or using a controlled substance is an essential element of the offense charged. . . . An act is done "intentionally" if done voluntarily and purposely with the intent to do something the law forbids, that is, with the purpose either to disobey or to disregard the law. . . . It is not sufficient to show that the defendant may have suspected or thought that the [property was] being used for [illicit drug activity]. . . .

As explained by the Federal courts, then, section 856 means what it says—the law only applies to defendants who have actual knowledge that their property will be used for drug use and who intend that very outcome. As a result, section 856 could never be used—as some critics have irresponsibly suggested—against the promoters of a rock concert whose patrons include some who are suspected of doing drugs during the live music performances. In this way, section 856 is very different than other laws proposed which would impose a "reckless" standard—holding, for example, a concert promoter liable where they had reason to believe that drug use might occur.

For example, a bill introduced in the House would create criminal liability for anyone who "knowingly promotes any rave, dance, music, or other entertainment event, that takes place under circumstances where the promoter knows or reasonably ought to know that a controlled substance will be used or distributed." I disagreed with this approach because it would have replaced the high legal standard of section 856, on the books for 17 years, with a much lower standard where a concert promoter could be prosecuted for the illicit drug activity of patrons for which the promoter had no actual knowledge. When I wrote section 856 17 years ago, I and my colleagues required actual knowledge of illicit drug activity. Actual knowledge is still the standard today.

Unwitting Owners Will Not Be Prosecuted

Let me now briefly discuss the second prong under section 856, the requirement that the defendant make their property available "for the purpose" of illicit drug activity. Again, courts have interpreted this prong in a way to ensure that section 856 cannot be used against innocent property owners where some incidental drug use occurs on their premises. One Federal court started its discussion of the purpose prong by noting that "'purpose' is a word of common and ordinary, well understood meaning: it is 'that which one sets before him to accomplish; an end, intention, or aim, object, plan, project.'". . . Thus, Federal courts have noted that it is strictly incumbent on the government to prove beyond a reasonable doubt not that a defendant knowingly maintained a place where controlled substances were used or distributed, but rather that a defendant knowingly maintained a place for the specific purpose of distributing or using a controlled substance. Accordingly, the courts have interpreted that "purpose prong" of section 856 to prevent prosecution of defendants who knowingly allowed drug use on their property. In so doing, the courts have recognized that it's not enough to simply know that illicit drug activity is occurring on one's property; the property owner must be maintaining the property for that specific purpose. This is particularly true when section 856 is used against a "non-traditional crack house," such as a residence or business. In fact, a Federal appellate court reversed a section 856 conviction against a defendant who had allowed her son to deal drugs out of his bedroom. There was evidence that his mother, the defendant, assisted him in his drug dealing. While the court sustained her conviction under a count of aiding and abetting, it reversed her conviction under section 856, finding that while she knowingly allowed drug dealing on her property, the primary purpose of her apartment was as a residence, not as a venue for illicit drug activity. As the court observed: manufacturing, distributing, or using drugs must be more than a mere collateral purpose of the residence. "Thus, 'the "casual" drug user does not run afoul of [section 856] because he does not maintain his house for the purpose of using drugs but rather for the purpose of residence, the consumption of drugs therein being merely incidental to that purpose.' We think it is fair to say, at least in the residential context, that the manufacture (or distribution or use) of drugs must be at least one of the primary or principal uses to which the house is put.". . .

This analysis makes clear that section 856 cannot be used—as critics of my law claim—against a concert promoter for the incidental drug use of their patrons or against a homeowner for the incidental drug use of a guest at a backyard barbeque. Just as section 856 "[does not] criminalize simple consumption of drugs in one's house," . . . it cannot be used to prosecute innocent event promoters, venue owners, or other property owners for the incidental drug use of the patrons or guests.

Here is the bottom line: Section 856 has been on the books for 17 years and I'm unaware of it ever being used to go after a concert promoter, a venue owner, or a private citizen for the incidental drug use of their patrons or guests. Why? Because, as the Federal court decisions I have briefly reviewed today show, we wrote into law a high burden of proof to make sure that innocent actors don't get prosecuted. If you don't know, for example, that the guy renting your arena plans to sell drugs, you are off the hook. If you don't intend for the guy renting your arena to sell drugs, you are off the hook. And if you don't intend that the guy renting your arena do so for the specific purpose of selling drugs, you are off the hook.

So let's get our facts straight here. It is just not helpful for critics of section 856 to run around screaming that the sky is falling, when it has not fallen for 17 years and has no reason to start now. As stated earlier, innocent actors have nothing to fear from this statute and I intend to monitor the enforcement of the Illicit Drug Anti-Proliferation Act closely to make sure that it is used properly. If someone uses a rave, or any other event, as a pretext to sell ecstasy to kids, they should go to jail, plain and simple. But that sad reality should not prevent responsible event promoters and venue owners around this country from putting on live music shows and other events, just because some of their patrons will inevitably use drugs.

Club Drugs Cause Brain Damage, Coma, and Death

Glen R. Hanson

The following selection is an extract of the testimony of Glen R. Hanson delivered to the Senate Caucus on International Narcotics Control in 2001. Hanson states that despite popular portrayals of club drugs as harmless and fun, these drugs are dangerous and can cause long-term damage to the brain. For example, he argues that people who use Ecstasy suffer from depletion of the brain neurotransmitter serotonin, which is key in regulating mood, sleep, appetite, and other functions. Hanson also discusses the dangers of gamma hydroxybutyrate (GHB), a club drug that can cause coma and death. In addition, he outlines the risks of ketamine, Rohypnol, and methamphetamines—other drugs that are often abused in rave or club settings. Hanson is a professor of pharmacology at the University of Utah and has done extensive research on the neurotoxic properties of MDMA and amphetamines. He has also served as director of the Division of Neuroscience and Behavioral Research at the National Institute on Drug Abuse (NIDA).

Mr. Chairman and distinguished members of the [Senate] Caucus, thank you for inviting the National Institute on Drug Abuse (NIDA) to participate in this important and timely hearing that focuses on a category of drugs commonly referred to

Glen R. Hanson, statement before the U.S. Senate Caucus on International Narcotics Control, Washington, DC, December 4, 2001.

as "club or rave drugs." I am Dr. Glen Hanson, the newly designated Acting Director of NIDA, and am pleased to be able to represent NIDA this afternoon.

As the world's largest supporter of research on the health aspects of drug abuse and addiction, I will share with you today what NIDA-supported research is telling us about club drugs, particularly 3,4-methylenedioxymethamphetamine (MDMA). I will also discuss briefly what we know about other drugs, including methamphetamine, ketamine, rohypnol, and gamma hydroxybutyrate (GHB) that are also reportedly being used in rave, dance party, night club settings, and other social settings frequented by adolescents and young adults.

There is now substantial scientific evidence demonstrating that these drugs are not benign. In fact, studies conducted to date [2001] in both animals and more recently in humans overwhelmingly confirm that club drugs are not harmless "fun party drugs" as they are often portrayed. While users of "club drugs" often take some of these drugs for energy to keep on dancing or partying, research reveals these drugs can cause long-lasting negative effects on the brain, altering memory and other behaviors. "Club drugs" include a group of diverse compounds that are capable of producing a range of unwanted effects, including hallucinations, hyperthermia, paranoia, amnesia, unconsciousness, and, in some cases, even death. When used with alcohol, these drugs can be even more harmful. We have also learned that, like most other drugs of abuse, the "club drugs" are rarely used alone. "Polydrug use" appears to be the norm, especially among young "club drug" or "rave drug" users. It is not uncommon for users to mix substances such as MDMA for example, with both alcohol and GHB or to "bump" and take sequential doses of a drug or drugs when the initial dose begins to fade. This is confirmed by both treatment admission reports and medical examiner reports. Also, drugs that are sold to individuals as "Ecstasy" tablets frequently contain not only MDMA, but other drugs or drug combinations that can be harmful. Because of these drug combinations, it is extremely

challenging to anticipate with certainty all the potential medical consequences that can result from the use of these popular party drugs. However, despite the challenges that confront
us in studying such a diverse pharmacological group of drugs,
we have learned a great deal about each one of the compounds.

Because of MDMA's increasing fascination both to young
people and the popular media, and the fact that our research
on the long-term effects of this drug is progressing at a rapid
pace, I will discuss it first.

The Basics of Ecstasy

3,4-methylenedioxymethamphetamine, which is frequently referred to by the acronym MDMA, and also known on the street
as "Ecstasy," has both stimulant and hallucinogenic properties. While MDMA does not cause overt hallucinations, many
people report distorted time and exaggerated sensory perception while under the influence of the drug. It also causes an
amphetamine-like hyperactivity in people and laboratory animals and like other stimulants, it appears to have the ability to
cause addiction. Use of MDMA increases heart rate, blood
pressure and can disable the body's ability to regulate its own
temperature. Because of its stimulant properties, when it is
used in club or dance settings, it enables users to dance vigorously for extended periods, but can also lead to severe rises in
body temperature, referred to as hyperthermia, as well as dehydration, hypertension, and even heart or kidney failure in
particularly susceptible people.

MDMA is typically available in capsule or tablet form and
is usually taken orally, although there are documented cases
suggesting that more and more it is being administered by
other routes, including injection and snorting. MDMA's acute
effects typically last from three to six hours depending on the
dosage, with the reported average dose of MDMA being consumed by a user being between one and two tablets, with each
containing approximately 60–120 mg of MDMA. However,

much higher doses of five tablets and greater are not unusual. MDMA appears to be well absorbed from the gastrointestinal tract, and peak levels are reached in about an hour.

Ecstasy Damages the Brain

MDMA works in the brain by increasing the activity levels of at least three neurotransmitters: serotonin, dopamine, and norepinephrine. Much like the way amphetamines work, MDMA causes these neurotransmitters to be released from their storage sites in neurons resulting in increased brain activity. Compared to the very potent stimulant, methamphetamine, MDMA causes greater serotonin release and somewhat lesser dopamine release. Serotonin is the neurotransmitter that plays an important role in regulation of mood, sleep, pain, emotion, appetite, and other behaviors. By releasing large amounts of serotonin and also interfering with its synthesis, MDMA causes the brain to become significantly depleted of this important neurotransmitter. As a result, it takes the human brain time to rebuild its serotonin levels. For people who take MDMA at moderate to high doses, depletion of serotonin may be long-term. These persistent deficits in serotonin are likely responsible for many of the long-lasting behavioral effects that the user experiences and what concerns us most about this drug.

There is also ample evidence to show that MDMA damages brain cells. We know that even one dose of MDMA (10 mg/kg in rats) has the ability to decrease serotonin levels for up to 2 weeks. Through the use of brain imaging technology, we can also see that human MDMA abusers may have fewer serotonin-producing neuronal processes in the brain than non-users. Despite what we have come to know about the detrimental consequences of this drug, there are increasing numbers of students and young adults who continue to use MDMA and other "club, rave or designer drugs" at increasingly higher doses. Several of our Nation's top monitoring mechanisms, including NIDA's long-standing national survey of drug use among 8th, 10th and 12th graders, Monitoring the Future (MTF), and our Community Epidemiology Work Group (CEWG), as well as findings from the Substance Abuse Mental Health Service Administration's (SAMHSA) National Household Survey on Drug Abuse, and the Drug Abuse Warning Network (DAWN) Survey, are reporting that the use of club drugs, particularly MDMA, is increasing in popularity among high school and college students. The most recent findings from SAMHSA's 2000 National Household Survey on Drug Abuse, which was released in October 2001, also shows an increase in MDMA use, with about 6.5 million people aged 12 or older reporting that they tried ecstasy at least once in their lifetime; up from 5.1 million lifetime users in 1999. NIDA's new MTF findings will be released later this month [December 2001] and will provide us with a better percentage of drug use trends among our Nation's youth, which in turn will help assist in developing better prevention approaches.

The Dangers of GHB

What the research is revealing about another drug used by some of our Nation's youth, gamma hydroxybutyrate (GHB), is equally disturbing. GHB is a central nervous system depressant (CNS) that is manufactured in clandestine labs and is typically sold in clear liquid in small bottles at night clubs or raves and is often added by the capful to beverages, particularly alcohol, and consumed orally. It is also available in capsule form. The onset of action is within 15 to 60 minutes and the effects typically last from 1 to 3 hours.

Although the predominant effects of GHB are sedative, GHB can produce a wide range of pharmacological effects depending on the dose. At lower doses GHB relieves anxiety and produces relaxation. However, as the dose increases, the sedative effects result in sleep and eventual coma or, if the individual is left unattended, even death.

Overdoses tend to be more frequent with GHB than with

other "club drugs," especially when used in combination with alcohol. Reported GHB-related emergency episodes in the U.S. have increased dramatically in recent years, from 56 in 1994 to 4,969 in 2000, according to SAMHSA's DAWN Survey. Some emergency room physicians are reporting a withdrawal syndrome that appears in patients who have self-administered the drug in a consistent dosing schedule (i.e., every 2 to 3 hours) for several months. The symptoms, which may include anxiety, restlessness, insomnia, rapid heartbeat, nausea, and vomiting, may be alleviated under the proper medical supervision.

As our knowledge about GHB and its use patterns evolve, so do the number of questions that need to be further explored. For example, we need to know more about the basic pharmacology of GHB; what the long-term consequences (e.g., tolerance, dependence, withdrawal) of using it are; who is using it; and most importantly, how to develop effective prevention and treatment strategies for it.

Methamphetamine in Clubs

Another drug that I'll briefly focus on today is methamphetamine. Although methamphetamine is not often considered under the umbrella term of "club drugs," there continue to be populations that regularly abuse this powerfully addictive stimulant in the "club" scene.

Methamphetamine is a stimulant that has pronounced effects on the central nervous system. It can enter the bloodstream very quickly and can increase activity, decrease appetite, and cause a general sense of well-being. The effects of methamphetamine can last 6 to 8 hours. After the initial "rush," there is typically a state of high agitation that in some individuals can lead to violent and dangerous behavior. The long-term effects of this drug on the brain may be particularly damaging when taken at the high doses typically used by drug abusers. Methamphetamine has been shown in both laboratory animals and more recently humans, to be toxic to dopamine cells, meaning it can literally damage the nerve endings of human brain cells, resulting in cognitive impairments.

Methamphetamine is an inexpensive and highly addictive drug. Its heaviest use is in the Western states and in some rural areas elsewhere. While it remains the most common primary drug problem in Honolulu and San Diego, the drug does not appear to be generally increasing in popularity among young Americans throughout the country, although some indicators suggest pockets of increasing use in some cities.

We are attempting to develop more effective treatments for some of these addictions. For example, we will be starting a clinical trial of ondansetron (used to treat nausea and vomiting) in methamphetamine-dependent patients. This drug has some amphetamine-blocking properties in clinical pharmacology studies. Additionally, medications that have demonstrated some success in treating other ailments, such as bupropion, which is often used to treat depression, and selegiline, typically prescribed to treat Parkinson's disease, are currently being tested in Phase 1 clinical trials. Behavioral therapies also have shown promising results in treating patients who suffer from addiction to stimulants.

Other Club Drugs

Ketamine is another drug that is used in rave or club settings. Ketamine is a rapid-acting general anaesthetic. It has sedative-hypnotic, analgesic, and hallucinogenic properties and is marketed in the United States and a number of foreign countries for use as a general anesthetic in both human and veterinary medical practice. Ketamine is similar to phencyclidine (PCP), although ketamine is more rapid in onset and less potent. Its effects typically last approximately an hour or less, with the overt hallucinatory effects also being short-acting. However, the user's senses, judgment and coordination can be affected for up to two days after initial use of the drug and reports show that even three days after ingestion ketamine users continue to show persistent memory impairment and elevated psychotic symptoms. There have been significant increases in ketamine-related emergency department visits reported in this country between 1994 and 2000, increasing from 19 to 263, according to SAMHSA's DAWN Survey.

Rohypnol is currently licensed overseas, but not in this country, as an anti-seizure drug. It is an extremely potent benzediazepine and is typically sold as individually wrapped tablets that are colorless, odorless and tasteless when mixed in beverages and taken orally. Because of its ability to sedate and to cause amnesia, it has been used to diminish women's resistance to sexual assault, giving it the reputation of being associated with "date rape."

These are a few of the illicit drugs that are reportedly being used by some of our youth in social settings such as all-night dance parties, raves or night clubs.

Ecstasy Is Not Nearly as Dangerous as Many People Think

Rick Doblin

This selection is a transcript of an online chat with Rick Doblin, president of the Multidisciplinary Association for Psychedelic Studies (MAPS), which sponsored the first government-approved study (2004) of MDMA's medical potential to help victims of trauma. According to Doblin, there is no evidence that the dosages of MDMA used in therapy will cause any physical damage to the patients. He argues that while MDMA is not completely harmless, it is not as dangerous as antidrug propaganda would have the public believe. Doblin also discusses what he considers the scientific and government prejudice against Ecstasy, the ethics of research, and the general risks and benefits of MDMA use. Chat moderator Thomas Bartlett is a reporter for the *Chronicle of Higher Education*.

Question from Nick, U. of Washington: Previous research has (perhaps falsely) argued that use of MDMA can reduce serotonin [mood-regulator] activity levels in the brain. Have there been studies that have tried to establish a link between MDMA use and memory retrieval in the long run? If so, what are some significant results? Also, what are implications toward attention deficits (if any)?

Rick Doblin: The best controlled studies of MDMA and long-term cognitive processing (memory and executive functioning) demonstrated no clear association between serotonin levels and performance but some association between amount of MDMA consumed and performance. MAPS [Multidisciplinary Association for Psychedelic Studies] has helped sponsor the first MDMA/memory study in a population of MDMA users who had very minimal use of other drugs. This study has not yet been published and is being used as the basis for a large grant application to NIDA [National Institute on Drug Abuse]. I can say that there is no evidence that the amounts of MDMA used in therapy will cause any neurocognitive consequences. We are administering complete neurocognitive evaluations in the MDMA/PTSD [post-traumatic stress disorder] study pre and post.

Getting a Realistic Picture of the Dangers

Question from Pat Turner, U. of Edmonton: I found that only the first few times I used Ecstasy that it was more of a therapeutical experience. I've consumed about 30 pills over a 5 month period. The last time I used, I had 2 average strength pills over 4 hours (average dose) and I completely freaked out. The previous use, I had 8 assorted pills over about 12 hours and I had an amazing time flyin' high. My question is, Does your mood prior to consumption have any effect on the nature of the high? . . .

Rick Doblin: Yes, set (which includes mood prior to consumption) and setting play a major role in the nature of the experience. It sounds to me that you have some emotional issues that arose during the time you freaked out that should be looked at closely through non-drug psychotherapy or just regular introspection. Sometimes, the most valuable benefits can come from looking closely at the content of difficult experiences.

Question from Hank Baca, retired US Army Officer: Since about 1000 people a year die from aspirin use and approx 25 died from X [Ecstasy] use last year [2003], are we focused on the wrong drug?

Rick Doblin: To be fair, way more people used aspirin than MDMA. We shouldn't turn our Drug War guns on aspirin but should work to reduce the harms of both aspirin and MDMA through public health and harm reduction measures, not primarily through the criminal justice system. In other areas of life, we accept significant levels of risk. About 5 times as many people went to the emergency room last year [2003] from cheerleading than MDMA. About 35 people die on average per year from skiing and about the same number from scuba diving, yet these activities are considered to offer some benefits and are not criminalized.

Research Issues

Question from [moderator] Thomas Bartlett: I have one, Rick. Could you talk a bit about the use of animals in Ecstasy research? Several researchers I spoke to . . . expressed strong doubts about the ethics of using primates in these kinds of experiments. What do you think?

Rick Doblin: Personally, I believe that in some circumstances animal research can be ethically justified. That said, I don't think that a strong case can be made for the ethics of Dr. [George A.] Ricaurte's killing of about 28 squirrel monkeys and about 9 baboons in pursuit of evidence that MDMA hurt dopamine [muscle-control] neurons when there was already clear evidence from human studies that heavy MDMA users had normal dopamine levels. Dr. Ricaurte et al. failed to even cite this evidence in their original [2002] *Science* paper.

Question from Gale Gladstone-Katz, MAPS member: Have there been any experimental treatment/studies with MDMA (Ecstasy) on the treatment of schizophrenia, or other studies with regard to mental health? And what were the results? Any referral for further information?

Rick Doblin: No studies have been conducted on MDMA in the treatment of schizophrenia. Dr. Julie Holland, author of *Ecstasy: A Complete Guide*, would like to eventually conduct such

---

research. Now would be a good place to announce that we learned yesterday that DEA [Drug Enforcement Administration] has given Dr. [Michael] Mithoefer his Schedule I license for the MDMA/PTSD study! This means that the first study of the therapeutic use of MDMA has now been fully approved, about 18½ years since MDMA's recreational and therapeutic use was criminalized on July 1, 1985. Our next study, currently in the design process, will look at MDMA in the treatment of anxiety in end-stage cancer patients. Studies with MDMA in schizophrenia are years in the future due to limited resources.

Question from Janice Robarts Dillon, student, Kaplan College: My belief is that Ecstasy has far more repercussions for women than men. Do you find that this is true and can you confirm my beliefs with some examples?

Rick Doblin: I'm not sure that this is the case. The Phase I clinical trials with MDMA didn't suggest that women were particularly vulnerable more so than men.

The Risks Have Been Exaggerated

Question from Mike Taffe, The Scripps Research Institute: Rick, while much of your critique of existing preclinical research has merit, you frequently take a stance which might be described as the opposite pole to a Ricaurte. That is, in your efforts to establish that low doses are not likely to cause permanent damage, you seem to feel that there is NO risk at ANY dose. So with respect to a previous question, is, in your view, it possible that 8 typical pills consumed over a 12 hr interval would produce lasting, possible permanent alteration to the brain? If so, is this a likely outcome in your view? Or would it take a particularly susceptible individual, or other factors to produce such lasting impact?

Rick Doblin: I didn't mean to give the impression that MDMA is the one and only drug that is risk-free. As a preface to answering your question about the risks of brain alteration after 8 pills in 12 hours, I'd like to first make a distinction between brain changes and functional consequences. While we should be concerned and interested in brain changes, what matters most is functional consequences since brain changes may reflect negative, positive or no functional consequences. In the largest and best controlled PET [positron-emission tomography] study ever conducted in MDMA users [in 2003] . . . heavy MDMA users who had consumed 799 tablets on average and had abstained from MDMA for about 18 months were the same as controls in serotonin levels. Current users who had consumed 827 tablets on average had levels that were

 THE HISTORY OF DRUGS

Rick Doblin's Vision of MDMA's Medical Future

Rick Doblin, noted advocate of legalizing MDMA for medical use, also advocates careful regulation of the drug and public education about the potential dangers of the psychedelic.

Unlike some medical-marijuana crusaders, [psychedelics-as-medicine advocate Rick] Doblin freely acknowledges that therapeutic use is only the first step toward greater freedom, toward a policy that encompasses both the benefits and risks of psychedelic drugs to self and society. He even envisions a licensing process, in which people who have used psychedelics under supervision without incident and who have no history of mental illness get a license to buy and take the drugs independent of any physician or clinic. The government would provide neutral information about the dangers of drugs, and drug users would take it seriously, rather than ignoring the hyperbolic claims that currently issue from federal and state agencies. Users who abuse the drugs (and Doblin is clear that MDMA, like any drug, can be abused) would lose their licenses. It's a loopy idea, to be sure, but no more loopy than the idea of spending $18 billion a year to make sure that citizens get high only on alcohol, nicotine, caffeine and Prozac.

Gary Greenberg and David Malley, "Doctor X," *Rolling Stone*, April 26, 2001.

identical with controls in most brain regions and only 4–6% lower in two brain regions. I therefore do not think that it is likely that 8 pills over 12 hours are likely to produce permanent alterations to the brain but it is possible. New studies with more selective PET ligands are underway and the data from them is eagerly awaited. Dr. Ricaurte and others have convincingly shown in animals that MDMA can reduce serotonin levels in primates that persist at least for seven years. Interestingly, no evidence was presented that these animals were in any way functionally compromised.

Question from Thomas B. Roberts, Northern Illinois Univ.: Do you think the Federal government has also suppressed information about the positive possible uses of psychedelics the way they have supressed information about Ecstasy?

Rick Doblin: The federal government over the last three decades has made it exceptionally difficult, and for most of that period impossible, to conduct scientific research into the therapeutic use of psychedelics, not just MDMA. Government drug information dismisses evidence of therapeutic uses of psychedelics. Right now on the website of ONDCP (the Drug Czar's office) [Office of National Drug Control Policy], information about MDMA says that it once was used by therapists before it was illegal but that therapists abandoned that use after they learned that the MDMA experience was difficult to control and mind-altering. This is a laughable statement since the MDMA experience isn't that difficult to control and it was used precisely because it was mind-altering. In general, the federal government wants us to believe that illegal drugs possess only risks and no benefits.

Question from James Sybert, non-profit organization: Do you think that MDMA poses a greater risk to health than moderate alcohol consumption?

Rick Doblin: Moderate alcohol consumption is increasingly seen as offering some overall health benefits to users. Moderate MDMA use is probably similar in risk level to moderate alcohol use, both with minimal risks and probably overall more benefits than risks. When we think about the extent of binge drinking in high school and college students, I think a case could be made that, in actual practice, alcohol is more risky than MDMA.

The Future of Research

Question from Kristie Stoick, Physicians Committee for Responsible Medicine: Again focusing on the use of animals in research, do you think that scientists will begin to move away from the large amount of animal research done with illegal drugs, and try to focus on learning about the effects on and treatments for the species in question: humans? I think that this controversy sheds light on a big problem: many animals and dollars are being sacrificed on experiments that have no bearing on the realities of the drug war.

Rick Doblin: Yes, now that the FDA [Food and Drug Administration], IRB [Institutional Review Board] and DEA have all finally permitted the MDMA/PTSD study to go forward, I think we will increasingly focus on human research. Also, as PET technology improves, we will obtain better data from humans and need to use animal research less frequently. I was the first person that Dr. Ricaurte gave a spinal tap to in order to assess MDMA neurotoxicity since I felt then, and still do, that we mostly need human research. The interspecies scaling model that Dr. Ricaurte used is not very accurate (it predicted that use of what turned out to be methamphetamine in primates with a 20% mortality rate was equivalent to a common recreational dose regimen) so it is difficult to know what conclusions to draw from non-human primate research.

Question from Rich Byrne, Chronicle of Higher Education: Tom Bartlett asked about animal experimentation, and I'd like to ask about human subjects. The 20th anniversary of Ecstasy's explosion into a full-fledged subculture has come and gone. Are there longer-term studies of Ecstasy use in the pipeline, and any hint as to what they might contain?

Rick Doblin: Unfortunately, there are no efforts underway that I know of to investigate MDMA users who started using it in the 1970s or early 1980s. For some time, Dr. Ricaurte and others proposed a time-bomb theory that said that while functional consequences of MDMA were not obvious, such problems might become more visible after the combination of age-related serotonin declines and insult from MDMA. However, serotonin doesn't decline that much with age, unlike dopamine which declines to a greater extent. Studies with long-time MDMA users would be quite important and should be undertaken.

The Controversy over the Therapeutic Benefits of Ecstasy Continues

Linda Marsa

In 1985 it became illegal to possess, use, or manufacture Ecstasy. As a result, the psychotherapists who had been using Ecstasy as part of the treatment they provided patients no longer had legal access to the drug. However, researchers continued to debate whether Ecstasy provides therapeutic benefits when administered in a controlled setting, and a few doctors and psychologists secretly defied drug laws to give MDMA to their patients. In this selection, medical writer Linda Marsa describes the controversy over the possible psychotherapeutic uses of Ecstasy. She details the cases of people who were able to overcome severe depression and trauma by taking carefully monitored dosages of Ecstasy. She also points out a growing number of studies have shown that Ecstasy use can cause brain damage and chronic depression and anxiety. In 2004 the federal Drug Enforcement Administration granted permission to a small group of researchers to study the therapeutic effects of Ecstasy. Marsa is the author of *Prescription for Profits* and a contributing editor to *Popular Science* magazine.

Sue Stevens was severely depressed after her young husband, Shane, succumbed to kidney cancer in 1999. She took large doses of numbing antidepressants to get through the day, and conventional therapy didn't help.

Then, last fall [2000], the 32-year-old Chicago woman chose a more radical approach. She traveled to the West to see a psychologist whom she had learned was using the illegal drug Ecstasy for a handful of patients suffering from severe trauma. In a single session, under the influence of Ecstasy—a drug that combines the effects of a psychedelic and an amphetamine—she said she was finally able to come to grips with her grief.

"Somehow, I knew Shane was no longer hurting, which made it possible for me to let go," said Stevens, who hasn't taken any antidepressants since. "It was like a wire that was disconnected got reattached and jump-started the healing process. Even if this feeling was just an effect of the drug, it's what I needed to do to move forward." Anecdotal reports from other mental health professionals suggest similar results from Ecstasy, said Rick Doblin, president of the Multidisciplinary Assn. for Psychedelic Studies, a nonprofit group in Boston that funds psychedelic research. "There's a whole network of 30 to 40 people around the country—some are psychiatrists, some are psychologists—who risk their licenses to use MDMA [the chemical name for Ecstasy] with their patients," he said.

The Controversy over Medical Use of MDMA

Lester Grinspoon, a professor emeritus of psychiatry at Harvard Medical School who has studied psychedelics but is not among the therapists prescribing Ecstasy to patients, said the synthetic drug can "greatly accelerate" the therapeutic process. "It enhances one's capacity for insight and empathy, and melts away the layers of defensiveness and anxiety that impedes treatment," he said. "In one session, people can get past hang-ups that take six months of therapy to untangle."

Other doctors, however, contend that MDMA is too dangerous to justify its use for any therapeutic purpose. "There's no scientific evidence that MDMA is beneficial; it's all anecdotal," said Dr. George Ricaurte, an associate professor of neurology at the Johns Hopkins School of Medicine in Baltimore. Giving patients even one dose of Ecstasy, he believes, is unethical because of its potential to harm.

The intense but largely unknown scientific debate over MDMA's possible psychotherapeutic use has been overshadowed by the recent storm of publicity about the health risks of the drug. The news is filled with horror stories of kids overdosing on Ecstasy at all-night parties, of machine-gun shootouts over Ecstasy deals gone bad and of disturbing surveys that show it is the fastest-growing illegal drug in America.

Fueling concern over Ecstasy's safety has been a growing number of studies that suggest it may alter the brain, impair memory and concentration, dull one's intelligence, and cause chronic depression and anxiety. That has led Alan Leshner, director of the National Institute of Drug Abuse, to distribute thousands of postcards with images of brain scans labeled "Plain Brain/Brain After Ecstasy." Yet some credible researchers insist that Ecstasy may be a valuable therapeutic tool when used with professional oversight. They contend that critics have exaggerated the drug's dangers, using weak science to bolster their arguments.

"The issue has become so politicized that it's impossible to get a fair, objective hearing," said Dr. Charles S. Grob, director of Child and Adolescent Psychiatry at Harbor–UCLA Medical Center in Torrance [California]. Grob helped conduct government-sanctioned tests of MDMA on humans in 1995.

The Dangers of Recreational Use

There is one thing, though, on which both supporters and critics of Ecstasy can agree: The recreational use of the drug is dangerous. Some people take multiple doses of Ecstasy, and the drug is often adulterated with other substances to create a potentially toxic mixture. And Ecstasy is often taken with other illegal drugs in crowded, overheated dance clubs, where users can become severely dehydrated.

Some mental health professionals say that rampant street use of the drug has tainted the reputation of a potentially valuable tool for treating mental ills that are resistant to conventional therapy, including alcoholism, drug addiction and posttraumatic stress disorder.

In addition, studying the parts of the brain stimulated by mind-altering compounds like MDMA gives scientists insights into brain chemistry. This understanding can assist them in formulating more effective medications for mental ills.

The scientific community has long had an ambivalent attitude toward compounds like MDMA: tantalized by what they can teach us about brain circuitry and their therapeutic promise, but fearful of their possible adverse effects.

The Case of LSD

The history of LSD is a case in point. Lysergic acid diethylamide was devised in 1943 by Swiss chemist Albert Hofmann. Apparently, some LSD seeped through his skin while Hofmann was working with the chemical in his lab. While bicycling home, the scientist experienced the first documented "acid trip."

LSD's discovery fueled a flurry of research by scientists attempting to identify the brain regions stimulated by the drug. LSD also ignited interest in serotonin, a chemical messenger in the brain that we now know regulates mood, sleep, libido, impulses and body temperature.

When serotonin was first isolated from blood cells in 1947, scientists thought it just constricted blood vessels. Then researchers noticed that serotonin and LSD had common chemical structures, which suggested the two compounds had a similar effect on the brain. Suddenly, serotonin became the subject of intense scientific scrutiny because it was believed to play a role in mental illness and schizophrenia.

This research paved the way for the development of antidepressants such as Prozac, Zoloft and the class of antidepressants known as SSRIs, or selective serotonin reuptake inhibitors, which maintain high levels of serotonin in the brain.

"If LSD hadn't been discovered, it may have taken decades, not years, before we figured out what serotonin did," said David E. Nichols, a professor of medicinal chemistry and pharmacology at Purdue University in West Lafayette, Ind.

LSD also proved effective in treating alcoholism and heroin addiction in studies conducted in the 1960s in Canada and Europe, chalking up recovery rates in the 40% to 50% range—much higher than traditional treatments. But research abruptly ceased in the United States in 1966 when the federal government banned LSD.

MDMA Is Banned

Despite scientists' efforts to maintain secrecy, MDMA met a similar fate. First synthesized in 1912 by German chemists at Merck Pharmaceuticals, the compound is both a stimulant like cocaine, which means it can raise a person's body temperature, blood pressure and heart rate, and a hallucinogen. In 1976, after publication of the first scientific paper on MDMA's psychoactive effects on humans, psychotherapists quietly began experimenting with it. One estimate suggests that perhaps 500,000 doses of MDMA were dispensed by therapists during the late 1970s and early 1980s, said Doblin, of the Boston psychedelic research group. MDMA was hailed by these therapists as a "penicillin for the soul."

"It augmented therapy by enhancing communication and intimacy, and allowed people to access repressed feelings and memories in a nonthreatening atmosphere," said Grinspoon, who has taken MDMA and said it led him to "extraordinary" personal insights.

Psychiatrist George Greer, for instance, conducted more than 100 therapeutic sessions with MDMA in San Francisco and Sante Fe, N.M. According to Greer, use of MDMA helped ease the pain of a cancer patient and assisted the daughter of a Holocaust survivor to rid herself of "the concentration camp consciousness that had colored her entire life." Greer also used the drug in couples therapy. "Virtually every couple said their intimacy and communication was greatly improved," he recalled. "They were able to bring all the skeletons out of the closet without being afraid their partner would reject them or feel betrayed."

MDMA's development as a therapeutic aid was detailed in the early 1980s by one enterprising patient, who recognized its lucrative potential as a party drug. He renamed it Ecstasy, and the so-called "love drug" became popular on the college party scene. In 1985, the Drug Enforcement Administration banned the use, possession and manufacture of MDMA, and therapeutic research in the U.S. came to a halt.

Negative Conclusions of Research

Soon, reports about MDMA's dark side surfaced. University of Chicago researchers reported that people taking MDMA were sensitive to even minor changes in ambient room temperature and could easily get overheated, possibly resulting in severe dehydration and even death. Other experiments in laboratory animals indicated even one dose of the drug damaged the ends of serotonin neurons, though scientists still aren't sure if that's necessarily detrimental.

In studies involving primates, exposure to MDMA caused brain damage that was evident six to seven years later. In humans, the toll from chronic use seems even more disturbing. Tests done at Johns Hopkins University in Baltimore revealed that frequent MDMA users had subtle deficits in memory and concentration. Other studies suggested that habitual Ecstasy users didn't do as well on standard intelligence tests.

"The evidence is extremely compelling that MDMA is harmful," said Johns Hopkins' Ricaurte, who conducted many of these studies.

Other scientists, however, think the jury is still out. Part of the problem is that most experiments showing MDMA's deleterious effects have been done on habitual users who mix it with other illegal drugs. Or the research subjects have taken Ecstasy laced with other drugs. So identifying the actual source of the trouble can be tricky.

Does Ecstasy Cause Brain Damage?

An autopsy of a 26-year-old chronic Ecstasy user who died of a drug overdose is a good example. His family donated his brain to scientific research in hopes of learning about how Ecstasy alters the brain. Scans of slices of his brain revealed that serotonin levels were reduced by 50% to 75% of normal levels. Critics have used this information to argue that Ecstasy leaves the brain practically moth-eaten—a fact that is not yet supported by research.

Scientists do know that Ecstasy triggers the release of massive amounts of serotonin from its storage sites, which is why users experience a feeling of euphoria. Artificially flushing the brain with so much serotonin eventually depletes reserves of this crucial brain chemical. Consequently, after weekend drug binges, people often experience a profound emotional letdown—a condition known in the Ecstasy-drenched Rave scene as "the terrible Tuesdays."

However, the individual whose brain was autopsied used many other drugs and may have had an underlying psychiatric disorder, said Stephen Kish, a University of Toronto pharmacologist who conducted the autopsy.

Kish speculated that the [Ecstasy user's] severe serotonin depletion might have been a symptom of depression. Or it might have been due to the cumulative effects of the combination of drugs that he habitually ingested. Or perhaps it was simply a reaction to taking six to eight times the normal dose of Ecstasy, as he had done just before he died.

"There was an extraordinary amount of Ecstasy in his

bloodstream so we really don't know whether the damage was permanent or reversible," said Kish. "Still, the available evidence is pointing in the same direction. The question is: Do you want to play Russian roulette with your future?"

Contradictory Research Conclusions

Swiss researchers, however, found that there was no apparent brain damage in people who used chemically pure Ecstasy only a few times. In a study done last year [2000] of people who had never taken the drug, 10 subjects were given a single dose of MDMA while an equal number received a placebo.

A month later, researchers used a PET scan to take snapshots of participants' brain activity. The images revealed there were no changes in the serotonin neurons.

"It was a small sample, so I can't say with total certainty that MDMA isn't harmful," said Dr. Franc X. Vollenweider, a psychiatrist at the Psychiatric University Hospital of Zurich who led this study. "But what I can say is that if you use it a few times in a clinical setting, it won't do brain damage."

Moving Cautiously into the Future

There also may be some hard data soon on MDMA's ability to enhance conventional psychotherapy. Two studies are exploring whether Ecstasy can help people recover from traumatic events, such as rape, incest or physical abuse.

Scientists in Madrid have begun prescribing MDMA for rape victims who haven't responded to conventional counseling. Researchers believe the drug will reduce these patients' intense fears so they won't feel emotionally threatened in therapy sessions.

In South Carolina, scientists are seeking government approval to test the drug's effects on victims of rape and other assaults who have been diagnosed with post-traumatic stress disorder. They believe MDMA may help to overcome the key stumbling blocks in treating these victims.

"People who have been abused have trouble trusting others, which is a real impediment to establishing a therapeutic relationship, and reliving traumatic incidents can provoke incredible anxiety," said Dr. Michael C. Mithoefer, a clinical assistant professor at the Medical University of South Carolina in Charleston. "We believe that using MDMA will make it possible for them to work through their trauma without feeling their fears, and to trust their therapists."

Still, experts sound a cautionary note. "I'm not saying this type of research shouldn't be done," said Johns Hopkins' Ricaurte. "But this is a drug that has documented potential for abuse. So human experiments must be done in the most careful and clear-minded of circumstances."

The First Government-Approved Study of Ecstasy for Medical Purposes

Rick Weiss

In early 2004 the Drug Enforcement Administration (DEA) issued its first formal approval for a study to test MDMA on humans in an attempt to ascertain the therapeutic benefits of the
drug. In this selection Rick Weiss reviews the history of MDMA
and its advocates' long struggle to win government approval
for studies of the drug. Weiss describes the study, which will
be led by a South Carolina doctor who will treat twelve trauma
patients with carefully monitored doses of Ecstasy followed by
several hours of counseling. The DEA requires that the Ecstasy
used in the study be meticulously tracked and protected in a
safe with an alarm system. Rick Weiss is a science and medical reporter for the *Washington Post* and the winner of a 2002
Science in Society Journalism Award from the National Association of Science Writers.

Capping a 17-year effort by a small but committed group of
activists, the federal Drug Enforcement Administration [DEA]
has agreed to let a South Carolina physician treat 12 trauma
victims with the illegal street drug ecstasy in what will be the

first U.S.-approved study of the recreational drug's therapeutic potential.

The DEA's move marks a historic turn for a drug that has long been both venerated and vilified.

Ecstasy, also known as MDMA, is popular among casual drug users for its reputed capacity to engender feelings of love, trust and compassion. The government classifies it with LSD and heroin as a drug with no known medical use and high potential for abuse.

The First Legitimate MDMA Research

Although the study's approval is by no means a federal endorsement of uncontrolled use, it will give ecstasy's proponents their first legitimate opportunity to prove the drug can offer medical benefits.

"MDMA opens the doorway for people to feel deep feelings of love and empathy, which is the core of being human," said Rick Doblin, president of the Multidisciplinary Association for Psychedelic Studies in Sarasota, Fla., the nonprofit research and educational organization funding the trauma study. "We should be looking at that and learning from that."

As a result of the DEA action, sometime in the next few weeks the study's first participant—still to be selected—will check in for an overnight stay at an outpatient counseling center in the Charleston area. (Investigators have asked that the location not be precisely identified.) He or she will take 125 milligrams of 99.87 percent pure 3,4-methylenedioxymethamphetamine—probably the highest quality MDMA on Earth—synthesized by a Purdue University chemist.

Ecstasy Can Be Dangerous

Michael Mithoefer, the Charleston psychiatrist who will lead the research, emphasized that ecstasy is by no means a benign drug. Indeed, he said, on occasion it has proved deadly at all-night dance parties, or raves, where it is often consumed.

"The fact that we have good evidence that we can use MDMA safely in a controlled setting does not mean it is safe to take ecstasy at a rave," Mithoefer said.

The goal is to help people with debilitating post-traumatic stress disorder face the pain at the core of their illness, he said, and learn to work with it.

"Because of MDMA's reported ability to decrease levels of fear and defensiveness and increase the sense of trust, we hope that will be a catalyst for the therapeutic process," Mithoefer said.

The Long Battle to Legitimize MDMA Research

Advocates have been aiming for such a study since 1986. The Food and Drug Administration gave its blessing in November 2001 after long consideration and analysis of three human safety studies funded by Doblin's group. It was two more years before the study got the required approval of an independent science and ethics board.

The DEA's issuance last week [February 2004] of a Schedule 1 registration, which allows Mithoefer to administer the drug under the specific conditions of the study, was the last hurdle.

From all indications, it was not a decision made lovingly by an agency that has called ecstasy "one of the most significant emerging drug threats facing America's youth." But with all the other federal requirements met, the role of the DEA—whose responsibility is to prevent "diversions" of the drug—was limited to documenting that Mithoefer had a big enough safe bolted securely enough to the floor, a qualifying alarm system and a set of records that would ensure careful tracking of every speck of the stuff.

"Whether we agree with the study is not relevant," said Bill Grant, the spokesman for the DEA. "All the qualifications were met."

Even some of ecstasy's leading critics said they could abide by the study if regulators were satisfied.

"The key issue is that all potential subjects be fully informed of the risks," George Ricaurte, a professor of neurology at Johns Hopkins University who has studied the drug [and is known for his negative conclusions], wrote in an e-mail.

The History of Ecstasy

Ecstasy was popular more than 20 years ago as an aid to psychotherapy. Recreational abuse drew it to the attention of the DEA, which in the mid-1980s began regulating it.

A black market emerged, and millions of young ravers and others have since tried the substance, which can induce what enthusiasts describe as up to eight hours of empathic conversation, contemplation and energetic sociality.

Most users report no long-term negative effects, though some speak of fatigue or depression for a few days afterward. There is a heated scientific debate as to whether ecstasy causes significant, long-term damage to parts of the brain.

All experts agree that ecstasy on rare occasions causes a sudden, inexplicable and fatal form of heat exhaustion. That is one reason there will be an emergency room doctor and nurse outside the Charleston-area therapy room—where each patient will sit and talk for hours with Mithoefer and his wife, psychiatric nurse Annie Mithoefer.

How the Study Will Be Conducted

To be chosen for the study, the patients—all victims of assaults unrelated to combat—must have moderate to severe post-traumatic stress disorder unresponsive to other drugs and therapies, and will first engage in preliminary therapy sessions with the Mithoefers. Twelve participants will get the drug, and eight will get a placebo. Each will spend that first session talking, listening to music and lying on a couch as needed—

though study rules require that at a certain point each patient must engage in a discussion about the trauma that has left him or her debilitated.

Periodic physical, emotional and neurological checkups will continue for several weeks, followed by a second ecstasy session.

Marcela Ot'alora, who in 1984—before ecstasy's use was criminalized—took it under a therapist's supervision to help her deal with the aftereffects of being raped, lauded the Charleston study's approval.

For years, she had been unable to wait in lines or stand with her back to crowds because of a fear of being attacked, said Ot'alora, who today is a therapist in a western state that she asked not be revealed. Ecstasy had a profound effect, she said: "I think for the first time in my life I was able to have compassion for myself, and also felt I was strong enough to face something that was frightening without falling apart.

"It's not a miracle drug, by any means," she continued. "But it allows you to go into the trauma and know it is past, and separate it from the present."

She said she has not wanted to take the drug again, even though she still feels less than fully healed.

"It's almost like it showed me the path I needed to take," she said, "and I can do that on my own now."

How Drugs Are Classified

The Controlled Substances Act of 1970 classified drugs into five different lists, or schedules, in order of decreasing potential for abuse. The decision to place a drug on a particular schedule is based mainly on the effects the drug has on the body, mind, and behavior. However, other factors are also considered. The schedule is used to help establish the penalties for someone using or selling illegal drugs. On the other hand, sometimes a potentially valuable drug for treating a disease can be incorrectly scheduled, greatly hampering the exploration of its usefulness as a treatment.

Schedule of Controlled Substances

RATING	EXAMPLE
SCHEDULE I A high potential for abuse; no currently accepted medical use in the United States; or no accepted safety for use in treatment under medical supervision.	• Heroin • LSD • Marijuana • Mescaline • MDMA (Ecstasy) • PCP
SCHEDULE II A high potential for abuse; currently accepted medical use with severe restrictions; abuse of the substance may lead to severe psychological or physical dependence.	• Opium and Opiates • Demerol • Codeine • Percodan • Methamphetamines • Cocaine • Amphetamines
SCHEDULE III A potential for abuse less than the substances listed in Schedules I and II; currently accepted medical use in the United States; abuse may lead to moderate or low physical dependence or high psychological dependence.	• Anabolic steroids • Hydrocodone • Certain barbiturates • Hallucinogenic substances

Schedule of Controlled Substances

RATING	EXAMPLE
SCHEDULE IV A low potential for abuse relative to the substances listed in Schedule III; currently accepted medical use in the United States; limited physical or psychological dependence relative to the substances listed in Schedule III.	• Barbiturates • Narcotics • Stimulants
SCHEDULE V A low potential for abuse relative to the substances listed in Schedule III; currently accepted medical use in the United States; limited physical or psychological dependence relative to the substances listed in Schedule IV.	• Compounds with limited codeine such as cough medicine

Facts About Club Drugs

MDMA (Ecstasy) was synthesized by Merck, a German pharmaceutical company, early in the twentieth century. The drug is related to amphetamines and mescaline.

Ecstasy became popular as a club drug in the 1980s.

Club drugs are commonly associated with "raves," all-night dance parties usually held in rented locations and playing loud, throbbing techno music. The typical rave has an air of mystery, and even holders of advance tickets may not know the location until the last minute.

Club drugs were rarely sold by gangs or street dealers until the turn of the twenty-first century.

The most common effects of Ecstasy use are relaxing of inhibitions; warm feelings toward others; and a happy, relaxed sensation, or "buzz."

Possible serious physical effects of Ecstasy use include rising body temperature and subsequent dehydration, severe depression, and eventual memory loss or other changes in brain function.

There is still considerable debate in the scientific and medical establishments as to whether the risks associated with MDMA outweigh its possible usefulness as a therapeutic drug.

Gamma hydroxybutyrate (GHB) was sold over the counter as a body builder, usually in health food stores, during the 1980s but was outlawed in 1992. It has been used as a club drug since the 1990s.

GHB induces a sense of euphoria and relaxation. Possible serious effects include coma and seizures; nausea and breathing difficulties, especially when combined with other depressants; withdrawal effects such as restlessness, tremors, and severe anxiety; and memory blackouts.

GHB usually comes in the form of a clear liquid and is odorless and tasteless. It therefore can be dangerously mistaken for water.

Other club drugs include ketamine and Rohypnol, both of which are similar to GHB in appearance and effects.

Ketamine induces a dreamlike state often accompanied by hallucinations and sometimes delirium; possible serious effects include respiratory problems and high blood pressure. Rohypnol's best-known dangers are total incapacitation and subsequent memory loss.

Because of their incapacitating and amnesic effects, GHB, ketamine, and Rohypnol have all been implicated in cases of drug-related sexual assault.

Ketamine—unlike MDMA, GHB, or Rohypnol—is approved for medical use in the United States and is most commonly used by veterinarians as an anesthetic. Rohypnol is used in some countries to treat sleep disorders.

Nicknames for MDMA include Ecstasy, hug drug, love drug, Adam, E, XTC; for GHB: liquid Ecstasy, soap, easy lay, vita-G, Grievous Body Harm; for ketamine: special K, vitamin K; and for Rohypnol: roofies, rope, rophies, roach, date-rape drug.

CHRONOLOGY

1912
Pharmaceutical company E. Merck files MDMA patent in Darmstadt, Germany.

1914
MDMA patent is officially approved.

1924
A paper is published mentioning MDMA as an intermediate in chemical synthesis.

1953
U.S. Army Chemical Center experiments with MDMA at the University of Michigan.

1960
French researcher Dr. Henri-Marie Laborit synthesizes GHB.

1961
Dr. Cal Stevens of Wayne State University discovers ketamine.

Late 1960s
MDA, a close relative of MDMA, becomes popular for recreational use. Users begin calling MDA the "love drug."

Mid-1970s
MDMA becomes a regularly prescribed therapeutic drug.

1976
Dr. Sasha Shulgin begins experimenting with MDMA, taking voluntary doses.

1977
Great Britain outlaws MDMA use under the 1971 Misuse of Drugs Act.

1978
Dr. Sasha Shulgin, in association with David Nichols, publishes his first paper on human use of MDMA.

Early 1980s

Recreational MDMA use becomes widespread in the United States.

1983

First ravelike party is held in Spain.

1984

Impending legal restrictions on MDMA become a matter of controversy in the United States, as doctors request hearings in response to federal plans to outlaw the drug.

Mid-1980s

Dr. George Ricaurte begins his MDMA research.

1985

The Drug Enforcement Administration (DEA) holds its first MDMA hearings in Washington, D.C. MDMA is placed under a one-year Schedule I ban (no recognized legitimate use outside of government-approved research).

1986

A DEA administrative law judge recommends MDMA be placed in Schedule III (certain legitimate medical uses). The newly founded Multidisciplinary Association for Psychedelic Studies (MAPS) opens a Drug Master File on MDMA.

1987

MDMA is briefly removed from Schedule I. Five Ecstasy-associated fatalities are reported. Manchester, England, sees its first raves. The First Circuit Court of Appeals in Boston hears the case of *Lester Grinspoon, M.D., v. DEA* regarding MDMA's legal status.

1988

MDMA is removed from Schedule I early in the year but returned in March. The "Summer of Love" takes place in Great Britain.

1989

British outdoor raves grow in popularity.

1990

The Federal Drug Administration bans over-the-counter sales of GHB in the United States.

1991
Early U.S. rave is held in San Francisco.

1992
FDA allows Dr. Charles Grob to use MDMA in clinical research.

1993
Great Britain adopts the Safer Dancing Campaign.

1994
Dr. Charles Grob begins human MDMA research at UCLA.

1995
Eighteen-year-old Englishwoman Leah Betts dies of physical trauma apparently caused by drinking excessive water in an attempt to dilute a dose of Ecstasy; the case provokes a storm of protest against the drug.

1996
Dr. Sasha Shulgin loses his license to work with Schedule I drugs.

1997
GHB becomes a Schedule I drug in eight states.

1998
Dr. George Ricaurte publishes a study indicating that MDMA use may impede the function of mood-regulating serotonin, sparking major controversy over whether the drug causes brain damage.

1999
The National Institute on Drug Abuse issues "Community Drug Alert on Club Drugs" and launches a $54 million multimedia campaign to educate the public on the dangers of club drugs. Ketamine is added to Schedule III.

2000
The Club Drug Act becomes law.

2001
A study published by researchers at Case Western Reserve University of Medicine suggests that MDMA taken by a pregnant woman causes long-term brain damage in her fetus.

2002

The RAVE Act is introduced in Congress. *Science* publishes a Johns Hopkins University study, by Dr. George Ricaurte, indicating that MDMA may contribute to Parkinson's disease.

2003

A revised RAVE Act passes as the Illicit Drug Anti-Proliferation Act. Dr. George Ricaurte retracts his 2002 study, admitting that the wrong drug was used in the experiments.

2004

The FDA approves a South Carolina study of MDMA's therapeutic effects.

2005

Police in Windsor, Canada, seize a drug shipment including a record 26,911 Ecstasy pills.

ORGANIZATIONS TO CONTACT

American Civil Liberties Union (ACLU)
125 Broad St., 18th Fl., New York, NY 10004
(888) 567-ACLU
Web site: www.aclu.org

The American Civil Liberties Union was founded in 1920 as a "guardian of liberty . . . to defend and preserve the individual rights and liberties guaranteed to every person in this country by the Constitution and laws of the United States [and] to conserve America's original civic values—the Constitution and the Bill of Rights." The organization is active in legal and community work in support of free speech, equal rights, and fair treatment for minorities as well as citizens' rights to due process of law and to privacy. Publications include *Drug Testing in Schools* and *Race & the War on Drugs*.

American Council for Drug Education (ACDE)
164 W. Seventy-fourth St., New York, NY 10023
(800) 488-3784 • fax: (212) 595-2553
e-mail: acde@phoenixhouse.org • Web site: www.acde.org

The American Council for Drug Education informs the public about the harmful effects of abusing drugs and alcohol. It gives the public access to scientifically based, compelling prevention programs and materials. ACDE has resources for parents, youths, educators, prevention professionals, employers, health-care professionals, and other concerned community members who are working to help America's young people avoid the dangers of drug and alcohol abuse.

DanceSafe
536 Forty-fifth St., Oakland, CA 94609
e-mail: dsusa@dancesafe.org • Web site: www.dancesafe.org

DanceSafe was created as "a nonprofit, harm reduction organization promoting health and safety within the rave and nightclub community." It provides drug education and party-site screening for recreational drug users. The Web site provides drug information and health tips as well as links to the latest drug news.

Drug Enforcement Administration (DEA)
Mailstop: AXS, 2401 Jefferson Davis Highway, Alexandria, VA 22301
(202) 307-1000
Web site: www.usdoj.gov/dea

The DEA is the federal agency charged with enforcing the nation's drug laws. The agency concentrates on stopping the smuggling and distribution of narcotics in the United States and abroad. It publishes the *Drug Enforcement Magazine* three times a year. The DEA Web site includes fact sheets on various drugs and an explanation of the drug classification system.

Drug Policy Alliance
925 Fifteenth St. NW, 2nd Fl., Washington, DC 20005
(202) 216-0035 • fax: (202) 216-0803
e-mail: dc@drugpolicy.org • Web site: www.dpf.org

The Drug Policy Alliance is a merging of the Lindesmith Center, formerly the leading drug policy reform institute in the United States, and the Drug Policy Foundation, a nonprofit organization that advocated sensible and humane drug policies. These two organizations joined in 2000 with the objective of building a national drug policy reform movement. The alliance works to broaden the public debate on drug policy and to promote realistic alternatives to the war on drugs based on science, compassion, public health, and human rights. The Web site includes links to fact sheets, documents, and other Internet sources with information on hallucinogens and drug research.

Drug Reform Coordination Network
1623 Connecticut Ave. NW, 3rd Fl., Washington, DC 20009
(202) 293-8340 • fax: (202) 293-8344
e-mail: drcnet@drcnet.org • Web site: http://stopthedrugwar.org

Founded in 1993, this network has grown into a national and global organization including parents, educators, students, lawyers, health-care professionals, and others working for drug policy reform from a variety of perspectives. The network promotes an open debate on drug prohibition and focuses on such issues as the reform of sentencing and forfeiture laws and the legalization for medical use of current Schedule I drugs. The Web site features an extensive online library with links to research and articles about hallucinogens, including "Drugs and Mysticism" and "Therapeutic Applications of LSD and Related Drugs."

Harm Reduction Coalition (HRC)
22 W. Twenty-seventh St., 5th Fl., New York, NY 10001
(212) 213-6376 • fax: (212) 213-6582
e-mail: hrc@harmreduction.org
Web site: www.harmreduction.org

The HRC's stated mission is "reducing drug-related harm among individuals and communities by initiating and promoting local, regional, and national harm reduction education, interventions, and community organizing." It publishes the *Harm Reduction Communication* newsletter and other educational materials.

Heritage Foundation
214 Massachusetts Ave. NE, Washington, DC 20002-4999
(202) 546-4400 • fax: (202) 546-8328
e-mail: info@heritage.org • Web site: www.heritage.org

The Heritage Foundation is a conservative public policy research institute that opposes the legalization of drugs and advocates strengthening law enforcement to stop drug abuse. It publishes position papers on a broad range of topics, including drug issues. Its regular publications include the weekly *Policy Wire*, the Backgrounder papers, and the Heritage Lectures series.

Multidisciplinary Association for Psychedelic Studies (MAPS)
2105 Robinson Ave., Sarasota, FL 34232
(941) 924-6277 • fax: (941) 924-6265
e-mail: askmaps@maps.org • Web site: www.maps.org

MAPS is a research and educational organization that focuses on the development of beneficial, socially sanctioned uses of psychedelic drugs such as MDMA. MAPS helps scientific researchers obtain funding and government permission for psychedelic research on human volunteers and distributes the results of such research. It publishes the quarterly *MAPS Bulletin* as well as various reports and newsletters.

National Clearinghouse for Alcohol and Drug Information
11420 Rockville Pike, Rockville, MD 20852
(800) 729-6686
Web site: www.health.org

The clearinghouse distributes publications from the U.S. Department of Health and Human Services, the National Institute on Drug Abuse, and other federal agencies concerned with alcohol and drug abuse. Papers available through the Web site include "Pulse Check: National Trends in Drug Abuse" and "Prevention Alert: Did 'Sixties Parents' Hurt Their Kids?"

National Institute on Drug Abuse (NIDA)
National Institutes of Health
6001 Executive Blvd., Rm. 5213, Bethesda, MD 20892-9561
(301) 443-1124
e-mail: information@lists.nida.nih.gov
Web site: www.nida.nih.gov

NIDA supports and conducts research on drug abuse—including the yearly Monitoring the Future Survey—to improve prevention, treatment, and policy efforts. It publishes the bimonthly *NIDA Notes* newsletter, the periodic *NIDA Capsules* fact sheets, and a catalog of research reports and public education materials.

Office of National Drug Control Policy (ONDCP)
Drug Policy Information Clearinghouse
PO Box 6000, Rockville, MD 20849-6000
(800) 666-3332 • fax: (301) 519-5212
e-mail: ondcp@ncjrs.org
Web site: www.whitehousedrugpolicy.gov

The Office of National Drug Control Policy is responsible for formulating the government's national drug strategy and the president's antidrug policy as well as for coordinating the federal agencies responsible for stopping drug trafficking. Drug policy studies are available upon request. ONDCP reports include "National Drug Control Strategy: HIDTA 2004 Annual Report" and "National Synthetic Drugs Action Plan."

Partnership for a Drug-Free America
405 Lexington Ave., Suite 1601, New York, NY 10174
(212) 922-1560 • fax: (212) 922-1570
Web site: www.drugfree.org

The Partnership for a Drug-Free America is a nonprofit organization that utilizes media communication to reduce demand for illicit drugs in America. Best known for its national antidrug advertising campaign, the partnership works to reduce the attractiveness of drugs to children and to prevent drug abuse among youths. It publishes the annual *Partnership Newsletter* as well as monthly press releases about current events with which the partnership is involved.

Project GHB, Inc.
556 S. Fair Oaks #101-178, Pasadena, CA 91105
e-mail: trinka@projectghb.org • Web site: www.projectghb.org

Project GHB is dedicated to discouraging the use of GHB and other club drugs by educating young people about the dangers. The Web site includes case histories and information about club drugs. Project GHB publishes the *Project GHB Newsletter* and various fact sheets.

RAND Corporation
1776 Main St., PO Box 2138, Santa Monica, CA 90407-2138
(310) 393-0411 • fax: (310) 393-4818
Web site: www.rand.org

The RAND Corporation is a research institution that seeks to improve public policy through research and analysis. RAND's Drug Policy Research Center publishes information on the costs, prevention, and treatment of alcohol and drug abuse as well as on trends in drug-law enforcement. Its extensive list of publications includes the book *Sealing the Borders*, by Peter Reuter.

Reason Foundation
3451 S. Sepulveda Blvd., Suite 400, Los Angeles, CA 90034
(310) 391-2245, x3037
e-mail: feedback@reason.org
Web site: www.reason.org/board.html

This public policy organization researches contemporary social and political problems and promotes libertarian philosophy and free-market principles. It publishes the monthly *Reason* magazine, which contains articles and editorials critical of the war on drugs.

FOR FURTHER RESEARCH

Books

Department of Justice, *It Never Went Away: LSD, A Sixties Drug, Attracts Young Users in the Nineties.* Washington: Drug Enforcement Administration, Demand Reduction Section, 1991.

Jimi Fritz, *Rave Culture: An Insider's Overview.* Victoria, BC: SmallFry, 1999.

Leigh A. Henderson and William J. Glass, eds., *LSD: Still with Us After All These Years.* New York: Lexington, 1994.

Julie Holland, ed., *Ecstasy: The Complete Guide: A Comprehensive Look at the Risks and Benefits of MDMA.* Rochester, VT: Park Street, 2001.

Icon Group International, *The Official Patient's Sourcebook on Club Drug Dependence: A Revised and Updated Directory for the Internet Age.* San Diego: Icon, 2002.

Philip Jenkins, *Synthetic Panic: The Symbolic Politics of Designer Drugs.* New York: New York University Press, 1999.

Cynthia R. Knowles, *Up All Night: A Closer Look at Club Drugs and Rave Culture.* Geneseo, NY: Red House, 2001.

Cynthia Kuhn, Scott Swartzwelder, and Wilkie Wilson, *Buzzed: The Straight Facts About the Most Used and Abused Drugs from Alcohol to Ecstasy.* New York: W.W. Norton, 1998.

Mark A. LeBeau and Ashraf Mozayani, *Drug-Faciltated Sexual Assault: A Forensic Handbook.* San Diego: Academic Press, 2001.

Tara McCall, *This Is Not a Rave: In the Shadow of a Subculture.* New York: Thunder's Mouth, 2002.

Michele McCormick, *Designer-Drug Abuse.* New York: Franklin Watts, 1989.

Fiona Measham, Judith Aldridge, and Howard Parker, *Dancing on Drugs: Risk, Health, and Hedonism in the British Club Scene.* London: Free Association, 2000.

Frank Owen, *Clubland: The Fabulous Rise and Murderous Fall of Club Culture.* New York: St. Martin's, 2003.

Scott W. Perkins, *Drug Identification: Designer and Club Drugs Quick Reference Guide.* Mason, OH: Thomson Learning, 2000.

Simon Reynolds, *Generation Ecstasy: Into the World of Techno and Rave Culture.* New York: Routledge, 1999.

Fran Robinson, *It Didn't Happen.* Victoria, BC: Custom Multimedia Creations, 2003.

Michael Sunstar, *Underground Rave Dance.* Lincoln, NE: Writers Club, 2000.

Andrew Weil and Winifred Rosen, *From Chocolate to Morphine: Everything You Need to Know About Mind-Altering Drugs.* Boston: Houghton Mifflin, 1993.

Periodicals

J. Adler, "Getting High on Ecstasy," *Newsweek,* April 15, 1985.

Associated Press, "Law May Link Rave Promoters, Ecstasy: House Members Consider Making Rave Promoters Liable for Ecstasy Use," October 10, 2002.

D.M. Barnes, "New Data Intensify the Agony over Ecstasy," *Science,* February 19, 1988.

Collegian Editorial Board, "Few Complaints About RAVE Act," *Colorado State Collegian,* October 9, 2002.

Will Doig, "Chemical Warfare: The RAVE Act," *Metro Weekly,* October 8, 2002.

FDA Consumer, "Strictest Controls for MDMA," September 1985.

Paul M. Gahlinger, "Club Drugs—Myths and Risks," *American Family Physician,* June 1, 2004.

Winifred Gallagher, "MDMA: Is There Ever a Justifiable Reason for Getting High?" *Discover,* August 1986.

Kathryn Rose Gertz, "The Agony of Ecstasy," *Science Digest,* February 1986.

———, "'Hug Drug' Alert: The Agony of Ecstasy," *Harper's Bazaar,* November 1985.

Humberto Guida, "Ask the DJ/Evolution's Jon Sutton," *StreetWeekly,* October 3, 2002.

Roger Highfield, "Designer Drugs," *World Health,* June 1986.

Steven Hyden and Greg Bump, "Rave Promoters, Enthusiasts Defend the Events," *Post-Crescent,* September 19, 2002.

Amanda Kay, "The Agony of Ecstasy: Reconsidering the Punitive Approach to United States Drug Policy," *Fordham Urban Law Journal*, June 2002.

Joe Klein, "The New Drug They Call Ecstasy," *New York*, May 20, 1985.

Kurt Kleiner, "Why Not Just Say Yes?" *New Scientist*, August 9, 2003.

T. Leggett, "Youth and Club Drugs: The Need for a National Drug Database," *Crime and Conflict*, 1999.

Evelyn McDonnell, "Antirave New World," *Miami Herald*, September 18, 2002.

Donald G. McNeil Jr., "Study in Primates Shows Brain Damage from Doses of Ecstasy," *New York Times*, September 27, 2002.

Celia Milne, "'Club Drug' Ketamine Good for Plastic Surgery," *Medical Post*, October 8, 2002.

Dan Nailen, "Culture Vulture: Orrin's Charge on the RAVE Scene May Have Legal Hangover," *Salt Lake Tribune Columnist*, October 8, 2002.

P.J. O'Rourke, "Tune In. Turn On. Go to the Office Late on Monday," *Rolling Stone*, December 19, 1985.

Stephen Rae, "The Agony of Ecstasy," *Mademoiselle*, June 1989.

George Ricaurte et al., "Hallucinogenic Amphetamine Selectively Destroys Brain Serotonin Nerve Terminals," *Science*, September 6, 1985.

Patrick Rogers and Peter Katel, "The New View from on High," *Newsweek*, December 6, 1993.

Wyre Sententia, "Your Mind Is a Target," *Humanist*, January/February 2003.

Jack Shafer, "MDMA: Psychedelic Drug Faces Regulation," *Psychology Today*, May 1985.

Lorna G. Davies Silcott, "Drugs—Delight or Death?" *Listen*, April 2004.

Time, "The Next High," September 15, 1986.

Todd Zwillich, "US Drug Officials Support 'Rave' Crackdown Law," Reuters, October 10, 2002.

INDEX